# Mashup Case Studies

## with

# Yahoo!® Pipes™

Tony Loton

**LOTONtech**

www.lotontech.com

# Contents

## About the Author

Tony Loton graduated in 1991 with a BSc. Hons degree in Computer Science and Management. Since then he has worked as an IT consultant, course instructor and lecturer (including with the UK's Open University), and author. In 2004 he gained recognition as a Microsoft Certified Professional (MCP).

Tony has been published in numerous Java and .NET related IT journals, and on Microsoft's MSDN Developer Center, in addition to authoring books published by Wrox Press and Wiley. Since 2007 Tony's books have been published by his own company, LOTONtech Limited (www.lotontech.com), with assistance from Lulu (www.lulu.com).

Tony has a keen interest in business and finance, and how 'markets' operate. This bias shines through in some of the examples he presents.

## Acknowledgements

I'd like to thank all those who volunteered to review the original manuscript for this book; for no more reward than a mention here – and a free copy.

Special thanks as always to Debbie Loton – for her attention to detail as copy editor and proof reader, and for being my wife.

## About This Book
This book is all about developing web content mashups using the popular Yahoo! Pipes web-based development environment. It follows on from my introductory book "Working with Yahoo! Pipes, No Programming Required" (ISBN 0955676444) which is available at `http://www.lotontech.com/it_books.htm`. The previous book is recommended reading, but not necessarily required reading for those of you who find *Chapter 2 Yahoo! Pipes Quick Start* to be sufficient introduction.

The case studies in this book demonstrate a range of practical, innovative, uses for Yahoo! Pipes mashups. They have an entrepreneurial e-commerce flavor about them, in contrast with the usual leisure-oriented examples that you will find elsewhere for sharing photos, videos, and places visited.

The examples not only provide solutions relevant to the stated scenarios, but also demonstrate many not-so-obvious Yahoo! Pipes features and techniques that are applicable to other scenarios.

## Conventions
This font (Verdana) is used for the main prose of the book.

The font `Courier New` is used for screen text, buttons, code listings and other verbatim text.

# 1 About the Case Studies

In this first chapter I summarize the case studies that follow in the remainder of the book. For each one, I summarize the business problem(s) addressed by the case study along with the technical solutions to those problem(s).

## Case Studies

Each case study is comprised of a number of examples – so although there are only six case studies, there are twenty-three separate examples in total.

### Affiliate Marketing

Affiliate Marketing is a web-based marketing practice through which individuals or companies refer their web site visitors to other web pages that describe third parties' products and services – in exchange for a referral fee.

In this case study I show how a Pipe may be used to append an affiliate's unique affiliate id to web links leading to Amazon and other affiliate-enabled web sites. From a technical perspective I demonstrate the `Union` module, the `Regex` module, Pipe cloning, and invocation of an Amazon Web Service (AWS).

### Selling Online

The examples in this case study demonstrate how Pipes can provide links to items you have for sale in the Amazon Marketplace or on eBay, and how you can generate Pipe output including PayPal 'Buy Now' buttons. The Affiliate Marketing topic is revisited, this time from the point of view of a merchant looking to offer an affiliate scheme.

From a technical perspective I demonstrate the `Fetch Page` and `Fetch CSV` modules, and I show how to:

- Embed a Pipe's JavaScript Object Notation (JSON) output in a web page

- Capture Pipe input parameters using a HTML form

- Generate HTML content to be displayed in a web page

Price Comparison
Price comparison web sites seem to be very popular at the moment, at least in the UK. In this case study I devise Pipes to:

- Compare book prices on Amazon, Barnes & Noble, and potentially other web sites

- Compare product prices within, and between, Amazon and eBay

- Screen-scrape credit card comparisons from an existing financial web site

From a technical perspective, I demonstrate how one Pipe can utilize another Pipe – as a sub Pipe, or by invoking its URL. I also show how information can be *scraped* from an existing web page using the `Fetch Page` module.

Stock Traders 'Cockpit'
In this case study I move away from the e-commerce buying and selling of the previous case studies, towards buying and

selling of a different kind; of listed stocks, or more specifically of stock market sectors.

I use a combination of HTML web pages and Yahoo! Pipes to devise a 'cockpit'; which displays snapshots of sector charts to the left of the page, and related sector news stories to the right.

## Mapping

This case study shows how Office Locations (or any other geo-encoded locations, for that matter) may be output from a Pipe, to be displayed on a Google Map or by utilizing the Yahoo! Pipes Get as a Badge facility. The examples demonstrate how the Location Extractor module deduces location information from human-readable addresses.

## Mashup Integration

Yahoo! Pipes is not the only mashup technology on the block. You can achieve so much more – and increase the size of your mashups audience – by combining Pipes with other technologies such as Microsoft Popfly and Google Mashup Editor (GME).

This chapter provides concrete examples of how to combine Yahoo! Pipes with the other mashup technologies.

## Keeping the Examples Working

Many of the example Pipes and HTML (web) pages presented in this book are available online, as indicated by boxed text:

---

You can access the Pipe(s) developed in this example at:
`http://pipes.yahoo.com/lotontech/cs_ebay_seller_items`

You can access the Web Page(s) developed in this example at:
`http://www.btinternet.com/~lotontech/pipes/html/PipeJSON.html`

---

**Tony Loton**

Since the underlying Pipes source their data from URLs that might change in future, the examples may cease to function correctly over time. If this happens to you, contact us via the web site at `http://www.lotontech.com` and we'll do our best to correct the problem for you and for other readers.

# 2 Yahoo! Pipes Quick Start

The main purpose of this book is to present some innovative uses for Yahoo! Pipes in the form of case studies; not to teach you how to use the Yahoo! Pipes environment from scratch. If you are new to Pipes, this chapter will provide a quick-start guide that may be sufficient for you to reproduce and run the examples herein.

*If you need more help, my introductory book "Working with Yahoo! Pipes, No Programming Required" (ISBN 0955676444) is available as paperback or PDF from* http://www.lotontech.com/it_books.htm, *and from online book stores.*

## Sign Up and Sign In
You can access the Yahoo! Pipes home page by pointing your web browser at URL http://pipes.yahoo.com. At the top-right of this web page you should see links to Sign In with your Yahoo! ID or Join Now. If you have an existing Yahoo! ID or email address you can use that, or you can create a new account by clicking Join Now.

## Create a Pipe
The Pipes home page displays a prominent button labeled Create a Pipe, which you click in order to... create a pipe!

The Pipe Designer shown in Figure 1 comprises a canvas (the main pane), a module library (to the left), and a debugger pane (across the bottom).

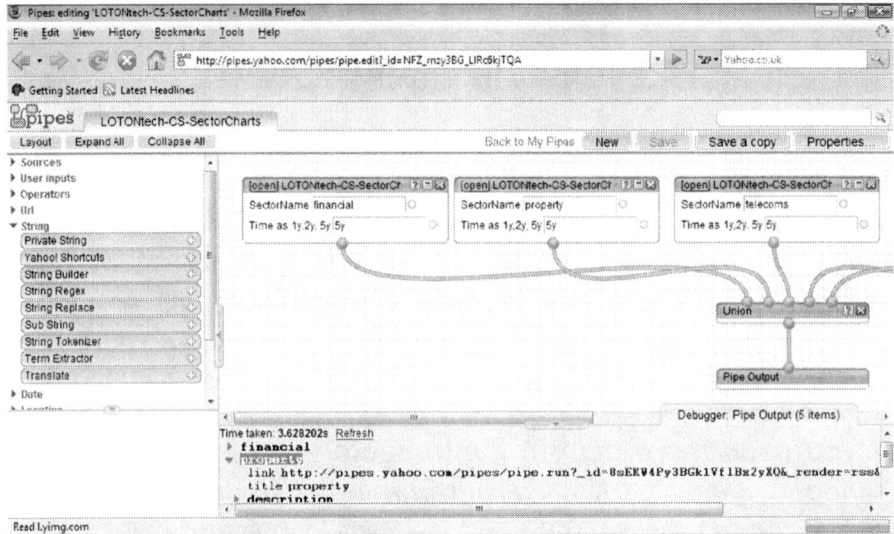

**Figure 1 Yahoo! Pipes Designer**

You create a Pipe by dragging modules or previously constructed sub Pipes from the library onto the canvas; by connecting the output terminal(s) of one module to the compatible input terminals of another module; and by making a final connection to the `Pipe Output` module that appears by default. Terminals are the circles that are shown around the edge of a module, or next to fields within a module.

The debugger pane shows the Pipe's output up to the point of whichever module is selected on the canvas. In the figure I have selected the `Pipe Output` module, so we see the final output of the whole Pipe.

## Save and Run

Buttons are provided across the top of the canvas, to `Save` or `Save a copy` of the Pipe. Upon saving the Pipe, a link appears for you to `Run Pipe`.

When you run the Pipe (Figure 2), a pull-down list of `More options` allows you to obtain the Pipe's output in various formats such as Really Simple Syndication (RSS) and JavaScript Object Notation (JSON). This will be important in later chapters.

**Figure 2 Run Pipe**

## Previously-saved Pipes

You can access your previously-saved Pipes at any time by clicking the `Back to My Pipes` link (in Figure 1) or the `My Pipes` link (in Figure 2).

Pipes that have been saved by other users may be accessed via their unique hard-to-guess URLs, examples of which you can see in the browser's title bar in those figures. A Pipe may also be given a friendly URL, thus the same Pipe may be accessed at:

```
http://pipes.yahoo.com/pipes/pipe.info?_id=NFZ_rnzy3BG_LlRc6kjTQA
```

or

```
http://pipes.yahoo.com/lotontech/cs_sector_charts
```

Many of the example Pipes presented in this book are available online, as indicated by boxed text like this:

> You can access the Pipe(s) developed in this example at:
> `http://pipes.yahoo.com/lotontech/cs_ebay_seller_items`

In most cases, my links will take you to a Pipe's info page (Figure 2) where you can see the Pipe in action. You will no doubt be interested in reviewing each Pipe's design (Figure 1), which you can do by clicking the `Edit Source` link.

## Summary

This chapter has provided a quick-start guide to how Pipes may be created, saved, and run. Now it's time for us to look at the first case study.

# 3 Case Study – Affiliate Marketing

Many online businesses generate additional, passive income by becoming marketing *affiliates*. As an affiliate, you provide hyperlinks from your web site through to related products or services offered by third parties. Each time one of your web site visitors clicks-through to the third-party's web site, or (depending on the scheme) makes a purchase, you earn a commission.

The third party knows that the referral has come from you because they will have provided an *affiliate id* that is encoded into each hyperlink as shown in the following examples:

```
http://www.taxcafebooks.co.uk/product.php?id=1234&prodid=ctr
```

```
http://www.amazon.com/gp/product/095567641X?ie=UTF8&tag=1234&linkCode=a
s2&camp=1789&creative=9325&creativeASIN=095567641X
```

Some affiliate schemes will tell you your unique id (or tag, in one of the above examples), and it's up to you to incorporate it into your links to the third-party web site. Some affiliate schemes will generate the links for you, and by analysing the link code – usually included in an HTML tag that begins `<a href="` – you can figure out your affiliate id.

Having set the scene by describing what an affiliate is, and how you are uniquely identified as an affiliate, how do I intend to make use of that information?

## Case Study Scenario

On my book-publishing web site at www.lotontech.com I list books written by myself and other authors, and I provide click-through links to booksellers (like Amazon) that offer the books for sale. As an affiliate of the booksellers, I'd like to capture a referral fee for the customers I introduce via my web site.

I'd like to create one or more Yahoo! Pipes that list my books with click-through links (incorporating my affiliate id). Using a Yahoo! Pipe will allow me to present the book list in various ways including: as a Pipe hosted by Yahoo! and searchable in their catalogue, as an RSS feed to which people may subscribe, and as a list embedded in my own web site.

## Mashup Implementation(s)

If you refer your web site visitors to third-party vendor sites as an affiliate or associate, the following Pipe implementations will help you automate the insertion of your unique affiliate id into hyperlinks.

### TaxCafe (Union example)

You can access the Pipe(s) developed in this example at:
http://pipes.yahoo.com/lotontech/cs_harcoded_affiliate_links

The simplest way to create a booklist with affiliate links is to concatenate a series of items in a Pipe. The Pipe design shown in Figure 3 uses an ItemBuilder module to create each item, with the RSS title and link fields set to the title of the book and the click-through link respectively. The Union module concatenates the items into a single feed.

I can run the Pipe by clicking the Save button followed by the Run Pipe... link, and I can then choose Get as RSS from the More options link on the Pipe's information page to give

Figure 4. The URL of the output web feed, which I can link to in my blog or email to my friends, is:

```
http://pipes.yahoo.com/pipes/pipe.run?_id=oB57fcvp3BGm8q_LouNLYQ&_rende
r=rss
```

The 'friendly' version of the URL is:

```
http://pipes.yahoo.com/lotontech/cs_harcoded_affiliate_links?_r
ender=rss
```

I could also embed the list in my web page by incorporating an `<iframe>` tag that has the above URL as its `src` attribute.

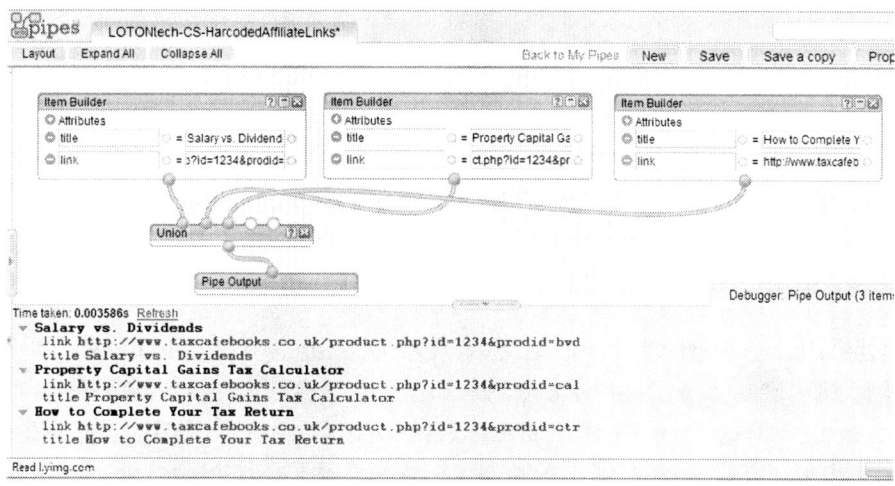

**Figure 3 LOTONtech-CS-HarcodedAffiliateLinks (Design)**

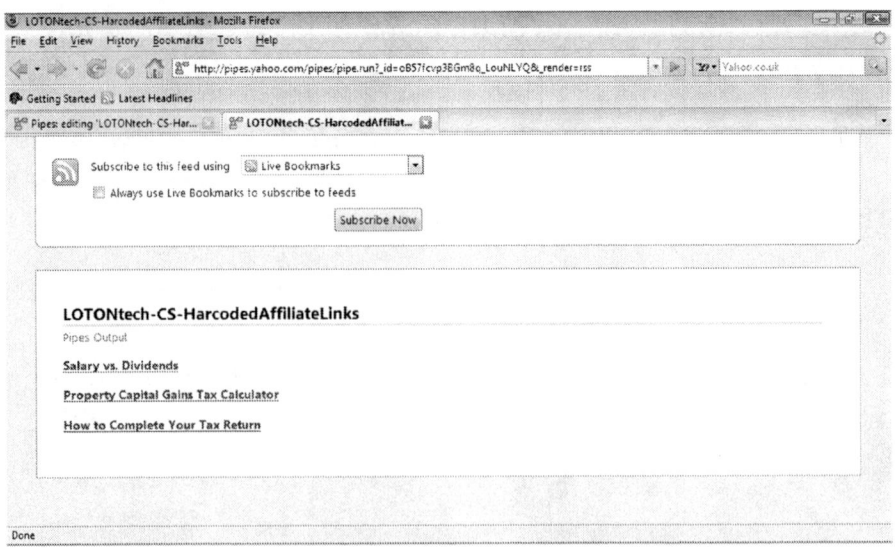

**Figure 4 LOTONtech-CS-HarcodedAffiliateLinks (RSS output)**

You might think "What's the point?" As a hard-coded list of books, I might as well have simply included the individual links in my blog, my email, or my web page.

The point is that I have defined the list in one place. If I modify the Pipe in future to include another affiliate-linked product, the new item will be visible automatically to my blog readers, web page visitors, and RSS feed subscribers.

## Lulu (ItemBuilder example)

You can access the Pipe(s) developed in this example at:
http://pipes.yahoo.com/lotontech/cs_append_affiliate_id_to_lulu_feed

Ok, so hard-coding the links might not be the best approach. A better approach would be to obtain a list of books from the bookseller dynamically, and to modify the bookseller links in order to incorporate my affiliate id. That's what I'll do in this example.

My books are available for purchase on the Lulu.com web site. I can obtain a full list of my books on Lulu, as a ready-made RSS feed, by following this URL:

```
http://www.lulu.com/browse/search.php?fOutput=rss2&fSearch=tony+loton
```

Each hyperlink in the feed links to a unique product page via a URL like this:

```
http://www.lulu.com/content/1750346
```

That's exactly what I want; an RSS feed that lists all of my books with hyperlinks to their individual product pages. The only problem is that the hyperlinks do not include my affiliate id, so Lulu won't be able to pay me a commission for each click-through.

I have solved this problem by designing the Pipe shown in Figure 5, which appends an affiliate id to each link URL of the input feed. Take a look at the figure, and I'll refer back to it as I describe each module.

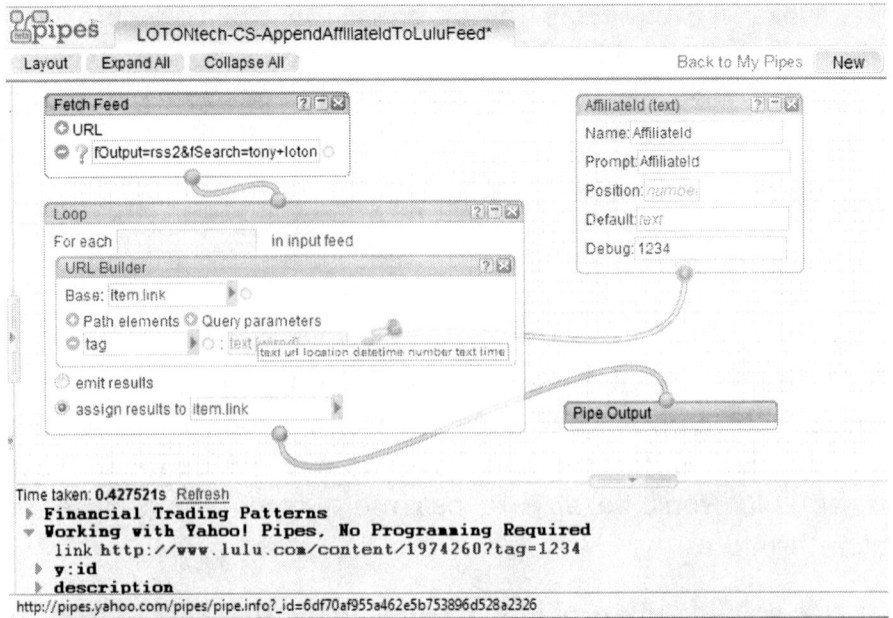

**Figure 5 LOTONtech-CS-AppendAffiliateIdToLuluFeed (Design)**

In this Pipe:

- A `Fetch Feed` module retrieves the input RSS feed from URL
  `http://www.lulu.com/browse/search.php?fOutput=rss2&fSearch=tony+loton`

- A `Loop` module loops through each item in the input feed, and executes an embedded `URL Builder` module for each.

- The `URL Builder` module takes its `Base` URL from the `item.link` element of the input feed, and appends a query parameter to the link URL so that:
  `http://www.lulu.com/content/1750346` becomes
  `http://www.lulu.com/content/1750346`**?tag=1234**

- While the name of the query parameter is hardcoded as `tag`, the value of the query parameter is actually wired up to the `Text Input` module titled `AffiliateId`. This means we can change this value to any affiliate id we like, at run time, without modifying the Pipe.

When I run this Pipe, it prompts me for an `Affiliate ID`. Alternatively I can incorporate this user input in the URL that I use to invoke the Pipe, like this:

```
http://pipes.yahoo.com/pipes/pipe.run?AffiliateId=1234&_id=6df70af955a4
62e5b753896d528a2326&_render=rss
```

If I type this URL directly in my browser, or email it to a friend, or post it to my blog, or incorporate it as the `src` attribute of an `<iframe>` in my web page, this is what will be seen (Figure 6).

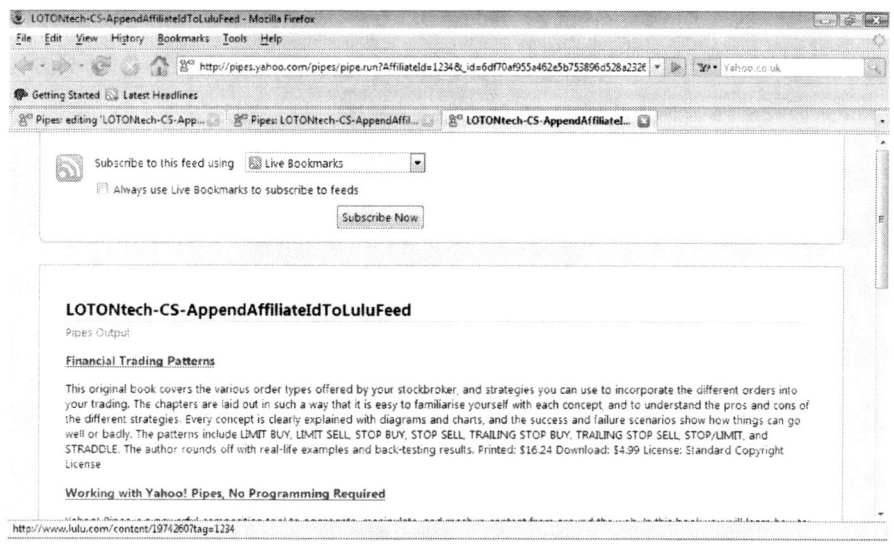

**Figure 6 LOTONtech-CS-AppendAffiliateIdToLuluFeed (RSS output)**

You might just be able to see at the bottom of Figure 6, that the link URL I have hovered over is `http://www.lulu.com/content/1974260?`**tag=1234.**

All of the hyperlinks in this Pipe's RSS output now incorporate my affiliate id, and I bet you can guess what happens if I run the pipe using the following URL:

```
http://pipes.yahoo.com/pipes/pipe.run?AffiliateId=9999&_id=6df70af955a4
62e5b753896d528a2326&_render=rss
```

You guessed it; now all of the hyperlinks in the Pipe's output are of the form `http://www.lulu.com/content/1974260?`**tag=9999**.

So not only have I created a Pipe that personalizes the Lulu.com feed of my books with *my affiliate id*, but I could now invite other people to use the Pipe to sell my books using *their affiliate id*. Except that Lulu doesn't really have an affiliate program, so this was a hypothetical example for demonstration purposes only.

## Amazon (Regex example)

You can access the Pipe(s) developed in this example at:
```
http://pipes.yahoo.com/lotontech/cs_append_affiliate_id_to_amazon_feed
http://pipes.yahoo.com/lotontech/cs_amazon_search
```

You will no doubt be aware that Amazon does have an affiliate scheme called *Amazon Associates*, so I'll use that as the basis of my next example.

I'd like to provide a list of links to my published books that are available for sale on Amazon, via a Yahoo! Pipe which appends my affiliate id to the links. The problem is that, as far as I know, there is no way to obtain an RSS feed of *my* books from Amazon. I can obtain a feed of Amazon bestsellers at the following URL, but what are the chances of me being in the bestseller list?

```
http://www.amazon.com/rss/bestsellers/books/ref=pd_ts_rss_link
```

Fortunately, I have a helping hand in solving this problem. Another Yahoo! Pipes user has created an Amazon Search Pipe at:

```
http://pipes.yahoo.com/pipes/pipe.info?_id=aAHDUL193BG8LFnqiXrL0A
```

You can see this Pipe running in Figure 7, in which I have entered values into the user input boxes to search for items mentioning `tony loton` (me), in Amazon's `Books` category, priced between `1` and `100` dollars.

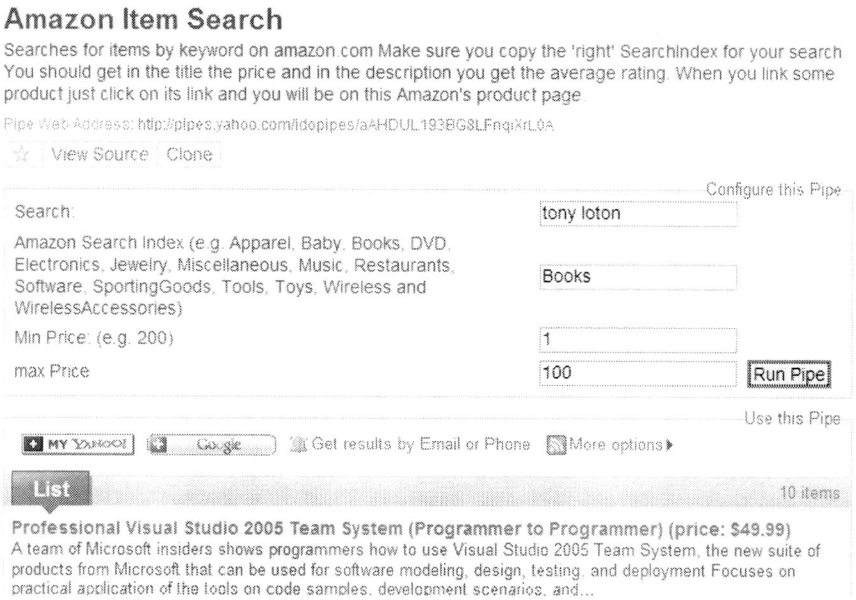

## Amazon Item Search

Searches for items by keyword on amazon.com Make sure you copy the 'right' SearchIndex for your search. You should get in the title the price and in the description you get the average rating. When you link some product just click on its link and you will be on this Amazon's product page.

Pipe Web Address: http://pipes.yahoo.com/ldopipes/aAHDUL193BG8LFnqiXrL0A

☆  View Source   Clone

Configure this Pipe

| | |
|---|---|
| Search: | tony loton |
| Amazon Search Index (e.g. Apparel, Baby, Books, DVD, Electronics, Jewelry, Miscellaneous, Music, Restaurants, Software, SportingGoods, Tools, Toys, Wireless and WirelessAccessories) | Books |
| Min Price: (e.g. 200) | 1 |
| max Price | 100   [Run Pipe] |

Use this Pipe

[+ MY YAHOO!]  [Google]   Get results by Email or Phone   More options ▸

**List**                                                                   10 items

**Professional Visual Studio 2005 Team System (Programmer to Programmer) (price: $49.99)**
A team of Microsoft insiders shows programmers how to use Visual Studio 2005 Team System, the new suite of products from Microsoft that can be used for software modeling, design, testing, and deployment Focuses on practical application of the tools on code samples, development scenarios, and...

**Figure 7 Amazon Item Search**

I'd like to take advantage of this pre-built functionality; so I copy the Pipe (notice the `Clone` link in the figure), I make a few changes so that it no longer asks for price parameters, and I rename it `LOTONtech-CS-AmazonSearch`. I won't show you the internals of this Pipe right now, because the point of this example is to treat it as black-box module that we can invoke from another Pipe.

The Pipe from which I will invoke this sub Pipe is shown in Figure 8. In this Pipe I:

- Include the sub Pipe LOTONtech-CS-AmazonSearch by dragging it onto the canvas from the My Pipes section of the Pipe Library at the left.

- Wire up the Search field of this sub Pipe to a Text Input module named Search Term.

- Add another Text Input module, which will allow me to specify the Affiliate Tag that I wish to include in each of the feed links.

- Wire up the output of the sub Pipe as the input to a Regex (Regular Expressions) module, which will insert my Affiliate Tag in the feed.

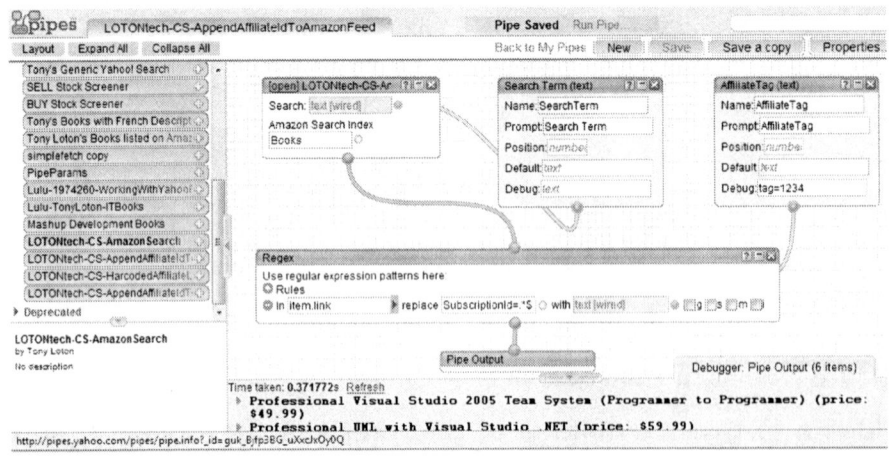

**Figure 8 LOTONtech-CS-AppendAffiliateIdToAmazonFeed (Design)**

The incorporation of my affiliate id is accomplished in a different way in this Pipe, compared with how the same thing was accomplished in my previous (Lulu) example. In this example, the Amazon Item Search sub Pipe produces links of the form:

```
http://www.amazon.com/gp/redirect.html%3FASIN=0764584367%26tag=ws%26lco
de=xm2%26cID=2025%26ccmID=165953%26location=/o/ASIN/0764584367%253FSubs
criptionId=1NVS1Q0GXRK4F68FV5G2
```

This link redirects Amazon to the specified `location` shown in bold. I'd like the redirect location to exclude the `SubscriptionId` parameter and include my affiliate tag, like this:

```
http://www.amazon.com/gp/redirect.html%3FASIN=0764584367%26tag=ws%26lco
de=xm2%26cID=2025%26ccmID=165953%26location=/o/ASIN/0764584367%253Ftag=
1234
```

I achieve this feat using the `Regex` module that supports a wide range of search-and-replace functions. In this module I want to modify the `item.link` so that I replace `SubscriptionId=.*$` (the text 'SubscriptionId=' followed by any number of characters until the end of the URL) with `tag=1234` (assuming that's what I specify as the `Affiliate Tag`).

*The Regex module provides Regular Expressions functionality. Regular Expressions are a subject in their own right, and I encourage you to find out more by visiting http://en.wikipedia.org/wiki/Regular_expressions.*

I can run my Pipe, specifying `tony loton` as the `Search Term` and `tag=1234` as the `Affiliate Tag`, as shown in Figure 9. Remember that I could also specify the inputs as query parameters by invoking the Pipe with a URL like this:

```
http://pipes.yahoo.com/pipes/pipe.run?AffiliateTag=tag%3D1234&SearchTer
m=tony+loton&_id=guk_Bjfp3BG_uXxcJxOy0Q&_render=rss.
```

It achieves pretty much what I want: a listing of all my books for sale on Amazon, each one linking to the item's product page via a URL incorporating my affiliate id. By clicking any one of the links, I can prove that the link URL is as I intend; for example:

```
http://www.amazon.com/o/ASIN/0764584367?tag=1234
```

```
http://www.amazon.com/o/ASIN/0764543768?tag=1234
```

I know what you're thinking – "But Tony, I'm not a book author or publisher".

Well, you can be an Amazon affiliate (or *associate*) without being the creator of the items you refer people to. If you happen to run a web site dedicated to mashup development, you can refer people to my books if you like. I don't mind because you'll get the referral fee, I'll get the royalty, and Amazon gets a cut too! Everyone's a winner!

On a more serious note, you should not take the book orientation of this example too literally. Take a look back at Figure 8 and figure out how you could adapt this Pipe to search Amazon's DVD catalogue, perhaps for films starring Kevin Bacon.

**Figure 9 LOTONtech-CS-AppendAffiliateIdToAmazonFeed (Run)**

I'll complete this example by satisfying your curiosity about the LOTONtech-CS-AmazonSearch sub Pipe.

In Figure 10 I show the design of the `LOTONtech-CS-AmazonSearch` sub Pipe. Not to give you a blow-by-blow account of every module – it's a black box, remember – but to draw your attention to the `URL Builder` module.

The author of the original Pipe, which I cloned, used the `URL Builder` in this Pipe to invoke an Amazon Web Service (AWS). This provides an example, then, of how you could design a Pipe to interact with a vendor's web service API.

In this case, the Pipe invokes the AWS `ItemSearch` operation so as to perform a product search. You will realize the true potential when I tell you that the AWS supports a wide range of functions as defined at:

```
http://webservices.amazon.com/AWSECommerceService/AWSECo
mmerceService.wsdl
```

By analyzing the Web Services Definition Language (WSDL) at this URL, you will discover that the range of available operations includes (but is not limited to) `ItemSearch`, `ItemLookup`, and `CustomerContentSearch`.

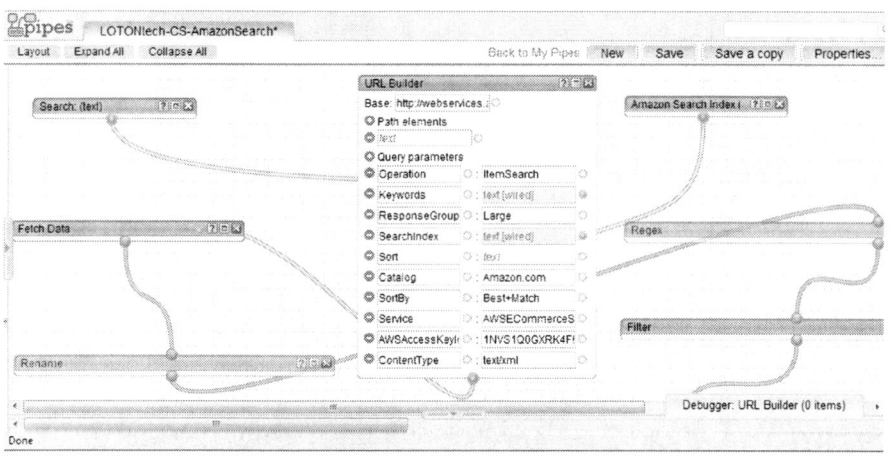

**Figure 10 LOTONtech-CS-AmazonSearch (Design)**

In order to use Amazon Web Services, you need to sign up at `http://www.amazon.com/gp/browse.html?node=3435361`. The author of the original Pipe had signed up, which is why he had an `AWSAccessKeyId` to enter as a `Query parameter` in the `URL Builder`. Although he has kindly (or foolishly) shared his access key with us, if you intend to invoke the AWS from your own Pipes then you really need to get your own.

One final point on the subject of invoking web services from Pipes: although the Pipes library includes a `Web Service` module, it is not necessary to use it in this case because the AWS accepts REST (Representational State Transfer) requests as described at:

`http://docs.amazonwebservices.com/AWSEcommerceService/20`
`05-10-05/PgRestRequestsArticle.html`

## Summary and Disclaimer

In this chapter I have demonstrated, in principle, how you could use Yahoo! Pipes in support of your *affiliate marketing* strategy. I say 'in principle' because I cannot guarantee that by employing these techniques as-is you will succeed in capturing the referral revenues that are due to you. The correct construction of referral URLs will depend on the particular affiliate scheme you use, and might change over time – for example, Amazon might decide in future that affiliates are identified by a tag such as `amazon_associate_id=[your id]`. So take my ideas as a starting point, adapt as necessary, and test the final solution to ensure that it achieves your objectives.

Finally, you should be careful to check that the automated construction of referral URLs is permitted under the terms of your affiliate agreement. Some affiliate schemes may mandate that you use only the links that they provide, unaltered.

Once you're happy on both these counts, have fun! And make money!

# 4 Case Study – Selling Online

Millions of people around the World sell things online; either professionally in the form of a business, as a hobby, or just to get rid of unwanted stuff. Some sell on the Amazon Marketplace, some on eBay, and some on their own web sites that take payment via PayPal.

In this chapter we'll look at how Yahoo! Pipes might be used in support of our online selling activities.

## Case Study Scenario

I sell information products (e-books) by listing them in the Amazon Marketplace, on eBay, and for direct sale on my own web site. I'd like to design a set of Pipes that list my items-for-sale along with 'purchase' links leading directly to the sales pages for the items.

The difference between this scenario and the one in the previous chapter is that in this case I am directing people to the sales pages for items that *I am selling*, rather than directing them to the description pages for items that *someone else is selling*.

So that you don't think this scenario is limited to my own information products, my eBay example relates to electronic products sold by another eBay seller.

As an extension of the direct-selling scenario, I turn the affiliate marketing idea from the previous chapter on its head. If I'm selling my own products, then why not offer my own affiliate scheme to interested parties? And provide each affiliate with a personalized storefront?

## Mashup Implementations

The following implementations demonstrate Pipes that generate hyperlinks to items you have for sale on Amazon, on eBay, or for direct sale via PayPal buttons. You will also see how you can embed Pipe results directly in a web page, and how you could use Pipes to support your own affiliate marketing program.

### Amazon Marketplace (Fetch Page example)

> You can access the Pipe(s) developed in this example at:
> ```
> http://pipes.yahoo.com/lotontech/cs_amazon_storefront
> ```

Although in the previous chapter I linked to my books on Amazon, in that case I'm not the one actually doing the selling. I get a royalty for each sale, and maybe a referral commission as an Amazon associate (affiliate), but still – I'm not the one doing the selling; Amazon is.

That's not the case when we consider the Amazon Marketplace, where anyone can sell new or used items provided they are in the Amazon catalogue. My paperback books are listed in the Amazon catalogue, and I use the Marketplace to sell PDF versions direct.

You can see the PDFs that I have for sale by visiting the LOTON*tech* Storefront at the following URL, and shown in Figure 11:

```
http://www.amazon.co.uk/gp/shops/index.html?ie=UTF8&sellerID=AOP6Y5VWYL
R6B
```

By clicking the Buy links next to the items on my storefront I can determine the URLs of each of the individual items-for-sale, which are:

```
http://www.amazon.co.uk/gp/offer-
listing/095567641X?seller=AOP6Y5VWYLR6B

http://www.amazon.co.uk/gp/offer-
listing/0955676428?seller=AOP6Y5VWYLR6B

http://www.amazon.co.uk/gp/offer-
listing/0955676401?seller=AOP6Y5VWYLR6B
```

Using this information I could create a Pipe with those links hardcoded, as I did in the *TaxCafe (Union example)* section of the previous chapter.

I would be able to present my web site visitors, blog readers, and RSS subscribers with a compact list of my book titles; each one linking directly the PDF purchase page. The list(s) would reflect any new (hardcoded) items that I added in the Pipe.

The only slight inconvenience is that, each time I made a new PDF available, I'd have to update my Pipe in addition to listing the item on the Amazon Marketplace. How much more convenient it would be if my Pipe could automatically determine the list of PDFs I have placed in the Marketplace.

Fortunately my storefront shows all of the PDFs I have for sale, so I just need a Pipe that can pick them out individually from that web page. This is exactly what my Pipe LOTONtech-CS-AmazonStorefront does, the design of which you can see in Figure 12.

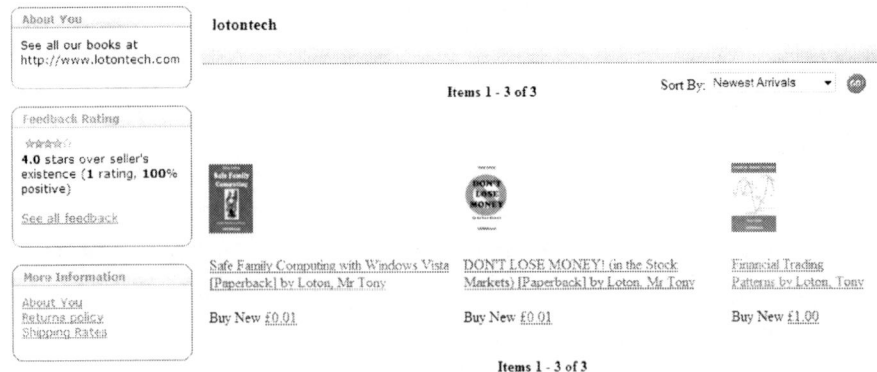

**Figure 11 LOTONtech's Amazon Marketplace Storefront**

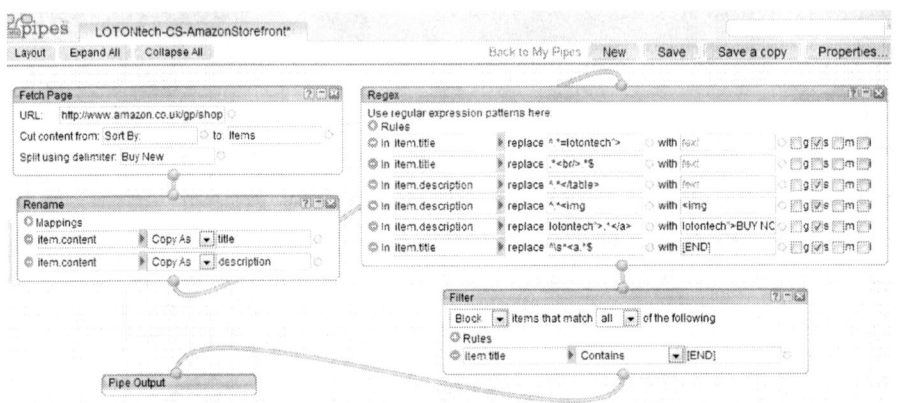

**Figure 12 LOTONtech-CS-AmazonStorefront**

Our starting point for understanding this Pipe is the HTML source code that underpins the Amazon storefront – which you can see for yourself by visiting the storefront page, right-clicking somewhere on the page, and choosing View Source or View Page Source (depending on your browser).

In Figure 11, notice how the list of items on the page is bounded by the text Sort By (above, to the right) and Items 1-3 of 3 (below). Below, I have reproduced the portion of the HTML source between those two bounds, with the bounding text shown in bold.

```
...
<form method=post action=/gp/shops/index.html border=0>
 <table border="0">
   <tr>
     <td class="small" style="vertical-align:bottom">Sort By:</td>
     <td>
       <select name="sortBy">
         <option value="StartDateDesc" selected >
                     Newest Arrivals
         </option>
         ...
       </select>
     ...
   </table>
</form>
...
<TABLE border=0 width="100%">
  <TR height="135">
    <TD valign="bottom">
      <a
href="/gp/product/095567641X?ie=UTF8&seller=AOP6Y5VWYLR6B&sn=lotontech"
><img src="http://ecx.images-amazon.com/images/I/01ydOndjNpL.jpg"
width="50" alt="Product image" height="75" border="0" /></a>
    </TD>
  </TR>
</TABLE>

<TABLE border=0 >
  <TR height="100">
    <TD valign="top">

      <a
href="/gp/product/095567641X?ie=UTF8&seller=AOP6Y5VWYLR6B&sn=lotontech"
>Safe Family Computing with Windows Vista [Paperback]  by Loton, Mr
Tony</a>
        Buy New
        <a href="/gp/offer-
listing/095567641X?ie=UTF8&seller=AOP6Y5VWYLR6B&condition=new">£0.01</a
>
    </TD>
  </TR>
</TABLE>
...
<table align=center>
  <tr>
    <td class=small valign='top'> <b> Items  1 - 3  of 3 </b>
    </td>
  </tr>
</table>
```

You will notice that I have also shown in bold the text **Buy New**, which serves to separate each item listed on the page.

The first module of my Pipe, `Fetch Page`, does exactly what I have just described. It fetches the storefront page, takes the portion between the `Sort By:` and `Items` text labels, and splits the page into a separate feed item every time it encounters the `Buy New` text. The debugger output from the `Fetch Page` module is shown in Figure 13; in which you can see there are three separate content items (one for each listed book), one of which I have expanded for illustration.

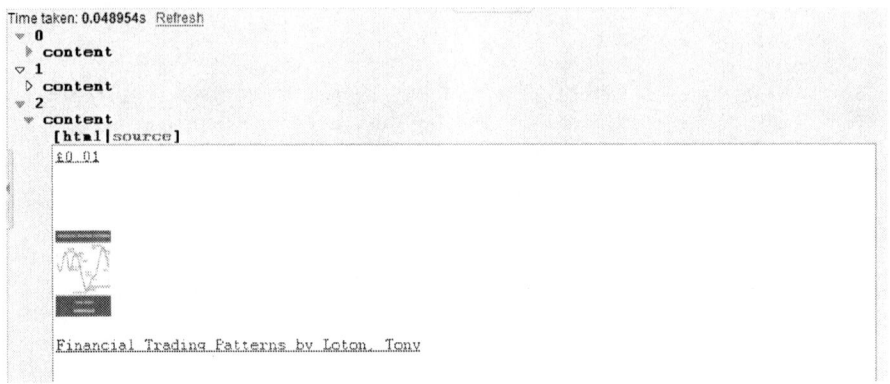

**Figure 13 Fetch Page output in Debugger**

In the next module of my Pipe (the `Rename` module) I take copies of each item's content into the title and description fields – which is necessary in order to see the output when the Pipe is run.

The next step is to use the `Regex` module to tidy up the `title` and `description` fields. In the `title` field I wish to remove all superfluous HTML and retain only the title text (shown in bold in the previous listing). In the description fields I wish to remove *some* superfluous HTML that resulted from the clumsy way in which the `Fetch Page` module split the page into separate entries. The regular expressions are as follows.

The first four regular expressions merely strip out superfluous HTML code from the `title` and `description` fields.

- In `item.title` replace `^.*=lotontech">` with *nothing*.

- In `item.title` replace `.*<br/>.*$` with *nothing*.

- In `item.description` replace `^.*</table>` with nothing.

- In `item.description` replace `^.*<img` with `<img`.

The next regular expression replaces the book's title, in the description's hyperlink (see Figure 13), with `BUY NOW` link text.

- In `item.description` replace `lotontech">.*</a>` with `lotontech">BUY NOW</a>`.

When I told you that the `Fetch Page` module splits the web page into 'three separate content elements', I wasn't telling the whole truth. Actually it produces four content items, the last one of which is superfluous. I use the final regular expression to identify this extra item and replace its title with the text `[END]`.

- In `item.title` replace `^\s*<a.*$` with `[END]`.

The final module in my Pipe, not counting the `Pipe Output` module, is the `Filter` module – which I use to filter out any items whose title is `[END]`.

Take note that I have formed `title` and `description` fields for each of the for-sale items on the web page, but no `link`

# Tony Loton

field. The `description` field retains sufficient HTML code for a product image and a hyperlink, as you can see in the Pipe's RSS output in Figure 14.

Clicking any of the BUY NOW links in this RSS output takes me to the item's Amazon product page in a mode that lists only me (`lotontech`) as the seller, as you can see in Figure 14. If I was really clever, I would also capture a referral fee on each sale by modifying the BUY NOW links to include my affiliate id (as described in the previous chapter).

**LOTONtech-CS-AmazonStorefront**

Pipes Output

**Safe Family Computing with Windows Vista [Paperback] by Loton, Mr Tony**

BUY NOW

**DON'T LOSE MONEY! (in the Stock Markets) [Paperback] by Loton, Mr Tony**

**Figure 14 LOTONtech-CS-AmazonStorefront (RSS output)**

**Figure 15 Amazon Product Page for LOTONtech Seller**

A word of warning for when you try out this approach for yourself: sometimes it can take a while for your Pipe design changes to be reflected in the Pipe's RSS output. If the changes you thought you'd made don't show up, just wait a while and then refresh.

## eBay (JSON in Web Page example)

> You can access the Pipe(s) developed in this example at:
> `http://pipes.yahoo.com/lotontech/cs_ebay_seller_items`
>
> You can access the Web Page(s) developed in this example at:
> `http://www.btinternet.com/~lotontech/pipes/html/PipeJSON.html`

Many people around the world sell new or unwanted used stuff on eBay. The great news is that eBay already provides RSS feeds, and any seller can get an RSS feed of his or her items for sale at this URL:

```
http://rss.api.ebay.com/ws/rssapi?FeedName=SearchResults&siteId=0&langu
age=en-US&output=RSS20&sass=yourSellerId
```

So, if your eBay seller id is `dijiworld`, you can get the RSS feed for your items-for-sale at the following URL, as shown in Figure 16.

```
http://rss.api.ebay.com/ws/rssapi?FeedName=SearchResults&siteId=0&langu
age=en-US&output=RSS20&sass=dijiworld
```

This RSS listing might be sufficient for your potential customers, as it may searched, sorted, and filtered; but it goes without saying that you could capture the feed in a Yahoo! Pipe and process it to your exact requirements. One possibility is that you simply want to make the feed more compact, by removing the price information and picture and retaining only the title of each item. Alternatively, you might want to transform the RSS feed into another format such as the JavaScript Object Notation (JSON).

I created a simple Pipe, with only a `Fetch Feed` module to fetch the RSS feed from the given URL. In Figure 17 I run the Pipe, and choose `Get as JSON` from the `More options` menu. Alternatively I could devise a URL to obtain the JSON output from the Pipe as follows:

```
http://pipes.yahoo.com/pipes/pipe.run?_id=pKarhVrr3BGtEAZ4jknRlg&_rende
r=json
```

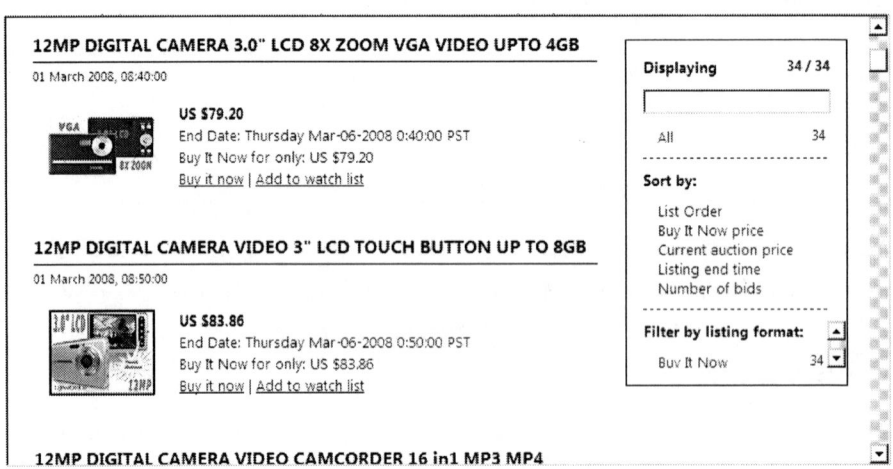

**Figure 16 eBay RSS Seller Listings**

**Figure 17 LOTONtech-CS-EbaySellerItems (Get as JSON)**

If I type the Pipe's JSON URL directly into my browser it will prompt me to save the output as a file, a portion of which I have listed below.

```
{"count":31,"value":{"title":"LOTONtech-CS-
EbaySellerItems","description":"Pipes
Output","link":"http:\/\/pipes.yahoo.com\/pipes\/pipe.info?_id=pKarhVrr
3BGtEAZ4jknRlg","pubDate":"Thu,      06      Mar      2008      00:58:56
PST","generator":"http:\/\/pipes.yahoo.com\/pipes\/","callback":"","ite
ms":[{"rx:ItemCharacteristic":{"xmlns:rx":"urn:ebay:apis:eBLBaseCompone
nts","content":"Listed                                             with
PayPal"},"link":"http:\/\/cgi.ebay.com\/12MP-DIGITAL-CAMERA-VIDEO-
CAMCORDER-3-0-LCD-8X-
ZOOM_W0QQitemZ320223214982QQcmdZViewItemQQssPageNameZRSS:B:SRCH:US:101"
,"rx:CurrentPrice":{"xmlns:rx":"urn:ebay:apis:eBLBaseComponents","conte
nt":"8386"},"y:id":{"value":"http:\/\/cgi.ebay.com\/12MP-DIGITAL-
CAMERA-VIDEO-CAMCORDER-3-0-LCD-8X-
ZOOM_W0QQitemZ320223214982QQcmdZViewItemQQssPageNameZRSS:B:SRCH:US:101"
,"permalink":"false"},"rx:AuctionType":{"xmlns:rx":"urn:ebay:apis:eBLBa
seComponents","content":"Buy                                        It
Now"},"rx:EndTime":{"xmlns:rx":"urn:ebay:apis:eBLBaseComponents","conte
nt":"1204794600000"},"description":"<table           border=\"0\"
cellpadding=\"8\"><tr><td><a     rel=\"nofollow\"     target=\"_blank\"
href=\"http:\/\/cgi.ebay.com\/12MP-DIGITAL-CAMERA-VIDEO-CAMCORDER-3-0-
LCD-8X-
ZOOM_W0QQitemZ320223214982QQcmdZViewItemQQssPageNameZRSS:B:SRCH:US:102\
">
```

To some of you, this JSON output will mean absolutely nothing – and is certainly not suitable for outputting direct to users. But the JavaScript programmers amongst you may well be getting very excited now.

One way to utilize the JSON output would be to use the jQuery library as described at http://www.seo-expert-blog.com/blog/parsing-yahoo-pipes-json-feeds-with-jquery.

It is also possible to write some relatively simple JavaScript code to display the JSON output in a web page. In the following HTML listing: the JavaScript code within the <head> tag provides a callback function that determines how each entry on the feed will be displayed, and the JavaScript code within the <body> tag specifies the pipe that should be run.

```
<html>

<head>

  <script type="text/javascript">

    function pipeCallback(obj)
    {
      document.write("<div><h3>Items for Sale on eBay</h3>");
      var x;
      for (x = 0; x < obj.count ; x++)
      {
        var buildstring = "<b><a href=" + obj.value.items[x].link + ">"
+
obj.value.items[x].title + "</a></b>. <span id=desc>" + obj.value.items

[x].description + "</span><br />";

        document.write(buildstring);
        buildstring = null;
      }

      document.write("</div>");
    }

  </script>

</head>

<body>
```

```
<script type="text/javascript"
src="http://pipes.yahoo.com/pipes/pipe.run?

_id=pKarhVrr3BGtEAZ4jknRlg&_render=json&_callback=pipeCallback">
  </script>

</body>

</html>
```

When I save this HTML code in file `PipeJSON.html` and open it in my Firefox browser, I am rewarded with Figure 18.

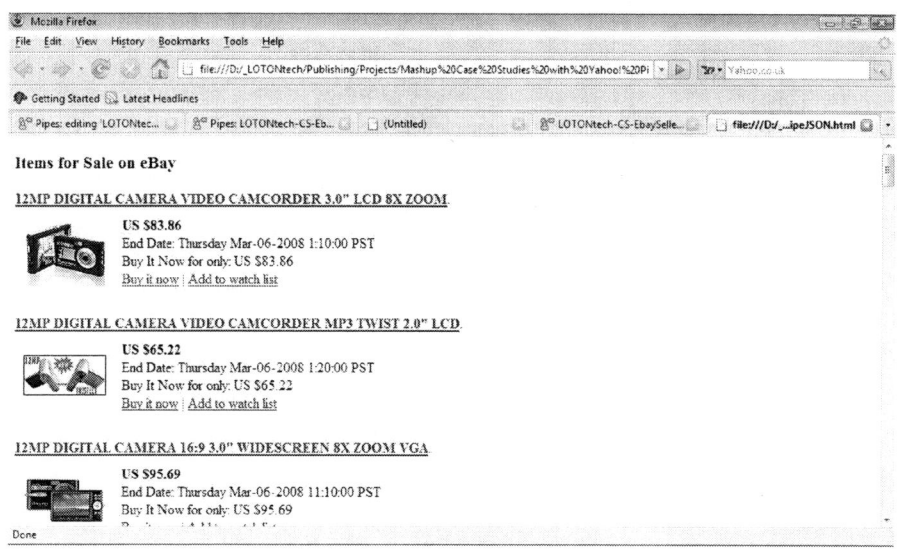

**Figure 18 PipeJSON.html (opened in Firefox)**

## PayPal (CSV example)

You can access the Pipe(s) developed in this example at:
`http://pipes.yahoo.com/lotontech/cs_paypal_links`

Like me, you may well offer items for sale on your web site for which you take payment directly via PayPal *Buy Now* buttons. If so, you could devise a Yahoo! Pipe that generates a list of items for sale – with PayPal buttons – from your electronic price list.

The starting point for this is to log in to your PayPal account and, within the `Merchant Services` tab, generate an unencrypted *Buy Now* button. The HTML that PayPal gives me for a button to sell my book "Working with Yahoo! Pipes, No Programming Required" would be:

```
<form action="https://www.paypal.com/cgi-bin/webscr" method="post">
<input type="hidden" name="cmd" value="_xclick">
<input type="hidden" name="business"
value="myemailaddress@somewhere.com">
<input type="hidden" name="item_name" value="Working with Yahoo! Pipes,
No Programming Required">
<input type="hidden" name="amount" value="5.00">
<input type="hidden" name="no_shipping" value="0">
<input type="hidden" name="no_note" value="1">
<input type="hidden" name="currency_code" value="USD">
<input type="hidden" name="lc" value="US">
<input type="hidden" name="bn" value="PP-BuyNowBF">
<input type="image" src="https://www.paypal.com/en_GB/i/btn/x-click-
but01.gif" border="0" name="submit" alt="Make payments with PayPal -
it's fast, free and secure!">
<img alt="" border="0"
src="https://www.paypal.com/en_GB/i/scr/pixel.gif" width="1"
height="1">
</form>
```

I'll use this code as a template, and I'll replace the values of the `item_name` and `amount` (shown in bold) on a per-item basis in my Pipe.

Next I upload my electronic price list as a CSV (Comma Separated Values) file to my web space as `http://www.btinternet.com/~lotontech/data/PriceList.csv`. The content of this file is:

```
TITLE, PRICE

Working with Yahoo! Pipes - No Programming Required, 5.00

Introduction to Microsoft Popfly - No Programming Required, 5.25
```

Obviously this file could contain as many entries as I like.

Now that I have a Buy Now button template, and an electronic price list, I can design my Pipe to combine the two. My Pipe comprises just four modules (plus the `Pipe Output` module) as shown in Figure 19.

The first module is the `Fetch CSV` module; which retrieves my price list file from its URL at `http://www.btinternet.com/~lotontech/data/PriceList.csv`, and which outputs the entries as separate feed items with fields mapped to the column headings TITLE and PRICE as specified on the first line of the file.

In the second module (`Rename`) I copy the `title` field into the `description` field. At this point a typical entry in the output feed would be:

```
title: Working with Yahoo! Pipes - No Programming Required
price: 5.00
description: Working with Yahoo! Pipes - No Programming Required
```

In the `Regex` module I replace the entire text of the description (`^.*$`) with my Buy Now button template string, which is:

```
<form action="https://www.paypal.com/cgi-bin/webscr"
method="post"><input type="hidden" name="cmd" value="_xclick"><input
type="hidden" name="business"
value="myemailaddress@somewhere.com"><input type="hidden"
name="item_name" value="[ITEM NAME]"><input type="hidden" name="amount"
value="[ITEM PRICE]"><input type="hidden" name="no_shipping"
value="0"><input type="hidden" name="no_note" value="1"><input
type="hidden" name="currency_code" value="USD"><input type="hidden"
name="lc" value="US"><input type="hidden" name="bn" value="PP-
BuyNowBF"><input type="image"
src="https://www.paypal.com/en_GB/i/btn/x-click-but01.gif" border="0"
name="submit" alt="Make payments with PayPal - it's fast, free and
secure!"><img alt="" border="0"
src="https://www.paypal.com/en_GB/i/scr/pixel.gif" width="1"
height="1"></form>
```

Notice that I have removed all newline characters to form a single unbroken string, and notice also that I have inserted place-markers `[ITEM NAME]` and `[ITEM PRICE]` where I intend the name and price of each item to go.

Output from the `Regex` module is fed into a `Loop` module, which loops through each item description and executes the `String Replace` module on each one.

The `String Replace` module replaces the `[ITEM NAME]` and `[ITEM PRICE]` in the description with the values `item.title` and `item.price` respectively, and assigns the results back to the `item.description`.

That's all there is to it, and the resulting RSS output is shown in Figure 20.

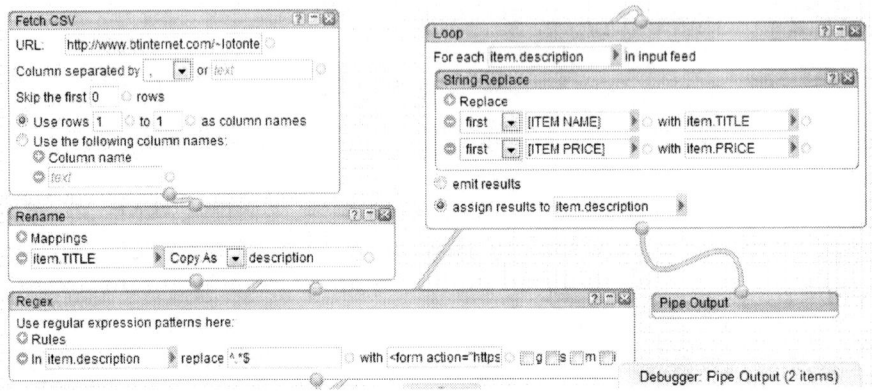

**Figure 19 LOTONtech-CS-PayPalLinks (design)**

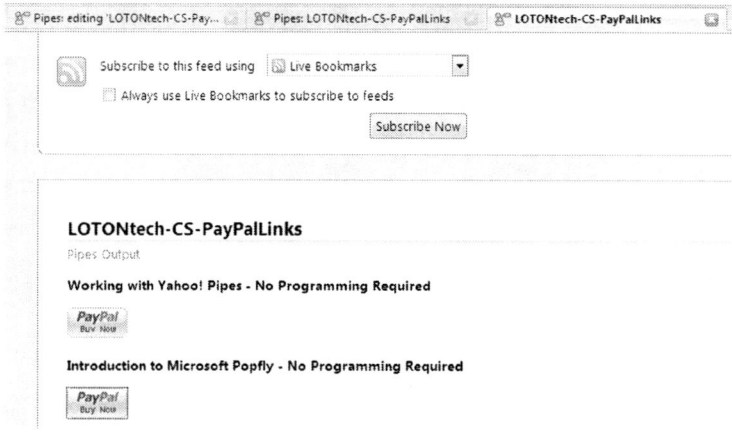

**Figure 20 LOTONtech-CS-PayPalLinks (RSS output)**

Clicking one of the Buy Now buttons in Figure 20 leads to the PayPal payment page for the relevant item. In Figure 21 you can see the PayPal payment page for Introduction to Microsoft Popfly - No Programming Required.

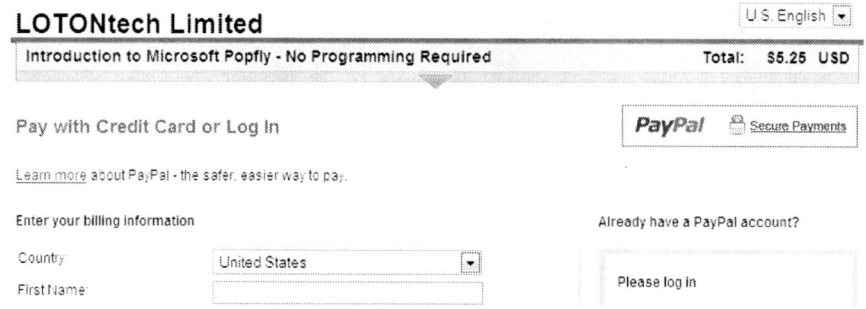

**Figure 21 PayPal Payment Page**

## Download Links (HTML Form example)

You can access the Pipe(s) developed in this example at:
http://pipes.yahoo.com/lotontech/cs_download_links

You can access the Web Page(s) developed in this example at:
http://www.btinternet.com/~lotontech/pipes/html/ProductDownloadForm.html

When I sell directly from my web site(s) using PayPal buttons, I am responsible for fulfilling the orders. Each time a visitor makes a purchase, PayPal sends an email detailing the item that has been sold, and I must then send the item (let's assume a PDF) by return email or by providing the purchaser with a link to the download page. The former is rather bandwidth-intensive because the PDFs might be several megabytes in size and will – I hope – be sold in large quantities. So how might I devise a Pipe to provide download links for a purchaser's items?

When someone first makes a purchase, I create a text file for that customer to detail their eligible downloads. Assuming the customer's name to be Rooney, I would create a file named `rooney.txt` and store it on my web space as `http://www.btinternet.com/~lotontech/pipes/data/customers/rooney.txt`. The content of this file would be:

```
ProductCode
Introduction to Microsoft Popfly
```

As each customer makes more purchases, their eligible download list will grow. So a customer named Beckham, who has made three purchases, might have file `beckham.txt` containing:

```
ProductCode
Safe Family Computing
Introduction to Microsoft Popfly
Working with Yahoo! Pipes
```

I've used meaningful names for illustration, but I could – of course – allocate a hard-to-guess customer id to each customer instead. Theoretically each customer could view his own eligibility text file, if he knew where to look, but could not modify it without knowing my web space password. Anyone could see the full list of text files by visiting the URL `http://www.btinternet.com/~lotontech/pipes/data/cus`

`tomers/`, but I could eliminate this possibility by including an `index.html` file in the web folder.

The next step is for me to create a download location for each PDF file, each at a hard-to-guess URL as follows:

```
Safe Family Computing at
http://www.btinternet.com/~lotontech/data/downloads/kjhg

Introduction to Microsoft Popfly at
http://www.btinternet.com/~lotontech/data/downloads/yrte

Working with Yahoo! Pipes at
http://www.btinternet.com/~lotontech/data/downloads/sdfk
```

The purpose of the Pipe will be to provide links to those download locations for a specified customer, according to the customer's eligibility. Look at the Pipe design in Figure 22, and then my description will follow.

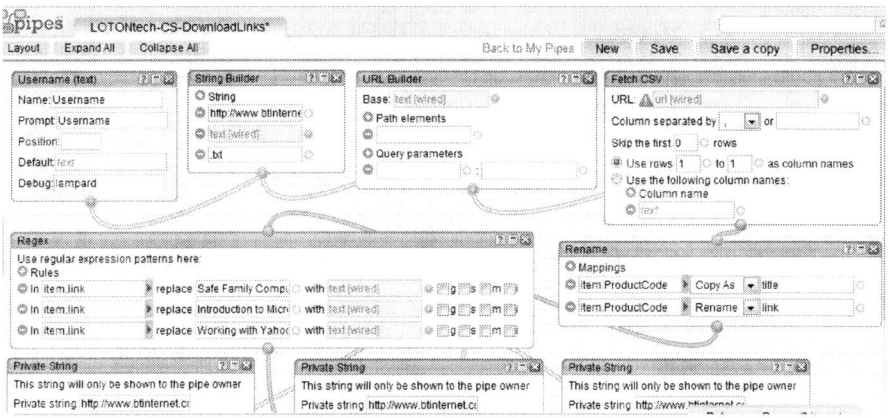

**Figure 22 LOTONtech-CS-DownloadLinks**

On the first row of modules this Pipe prompts for a customer username, builds a URL to the customer's eligibility text file (using `String Builder` and `URL Builder`), and reads the file using the `Fetch CSV` module.

On the second row of modules, I first use the `Rename` module to take copies of each text file entry (`item.ProductCode`) into fields named `title` and `link`. Next, I use the `Regex` module to replace the name of the product in each link with the product's hard-to-guess download URL; so, for example in the `link` field:

```
Safe Family Computing becomes
http://www.btinternet.com/~lotontech/data/downloads/kjhg

Introduction to Microsoft Popfly becomes
http://www.btinternet.com/~lotontech/data/downloads/yrte

Working with Yahoo! Pipes becomes
http://www.btinternet.com/~lotontech/data/downloads/sdfk
```

Note that I have not specified the hard-to-guess URLs in the `Regex` module itself, because that would allow anyone to discover the mappings by reviewing my Pipe design online. Instead, I have wired in these replacement strings from the `Private String` modules which allow only the Pipe author (me) to ever see what they are.

At this point, I could invite any customer to visit my Pipe and enter his or her username to reveal a list of eligible download links. It's not the most user-friendly interface for my purchasers, and in any case they need not know I'm utilizing Yahoo! Pipes, so I'll provide a web page as the front-end.

The HTML code for my 'Customer Downloads' web page at `http://www.btinternet.com/~lotontech/pipes/html/ProductDownload Form.html` is as follows:

```html
<html>
<head></head>

<body>

<form name="input" action="http://pipes.yahoo.com/pipes/pipe.run"
method="get" target="downloadsFrame">
Enter your Username to access your downloads
```

```
<input type="text" name="Username">
<input type="submit" value="Submit">
<input name="_id" type="hidden" value="eL0p1Znu3BGk_Qb1y6ky6g">
<input name="_render" type="hidden" value="rss">
</form>

<iframe name="downloadsFrame" width="600" height="300"/>

</body>
</html>
```

In this listing I use a HTML form to prompt for the customer's username. The form will submit to a URL comprising the form `action` plus the form's `Username` field and the `_id` and `_render` fields, like this:

```
http://pipes.yahoo.com/pipes/pipe.run?Username=beckham&_id=eL0p1Znu3BGk
_Qb1y6ky6g&_render=rss
```

The form's `target` attribute determines that the Pipe output should be rendered in the `<iframe>` named `downloadsFrame`.

The end results for customers `beckham` (three purchases), and `lampard` (two purchases), are shown in Figure 23 and Figure 24 respectively.

Although I have presented the download links using the Pipe's RSS rendering, I could alternatively have utilized the Pipe's JSON output as described earlier in *eBay (JSON in Web Page example)*.

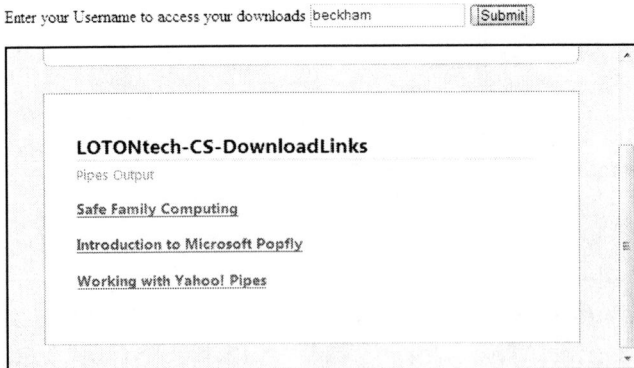

## Figure 23 Download links for 'beckham'

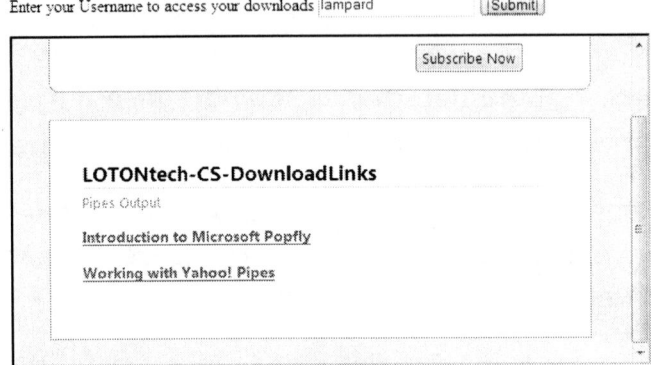

## Figure 24 Download links for 'lampard'

You should be able to try this for yourself at http://www.btinternet.com/~lotontech/pipes/html/ProductDownload Form.html

## Merchant Affiliate (HTML Serving example)

You can access the Pipe(s) developed in this example at:
http://pipes.yahoo.com/lotontech/cs_affiliate_page_content

You can access the Web Page(s) developed in this example at:
http://www.btinternet.com/~lotontech/pipes/html/PDFtechAffiliatePage.ht ml

In this example we'll return to the subject of Affiliate Marketing that was first covered in chapter *3 Case Study – Affiliate Marketing*. This time we'll look at it the other way around; that is, *you* offering an affiliate program to referrers rather than you participating as a referrer in someone else's program.

You may wonder why I present this example here, rather than in the other chapter. Firstly, it's because, in this example, you will be doing the actual selling of the items to the referred customers. Secondly, this example builds on this chapter's previous two examples: *PayPal (CSV example)* and *Download Links (HTML Form example)*.

Affiliate programs usually provide the referrer with some kind of personalized storefront which lists the vendor's items but which is somehow *branded* with the referrer's name. For example: Amazon allows referrers to establish an aStore (see mine at `http://astore.amazon.com/10a6f-20`), and Tax Cafe UK provide them with a Tax Bookshop (see mine at `http://www.taxcafebooks.co.uk/index.php?id=11263`). The purpose of this example is to provide referring affiliates with this kind of personalized storefront.

The whole point of an affiliate storefront is to provide purchase links or buttons that somehow incorporate the referrer's unique id. I'll create some PayPal buttons, pretty much as I did in *PayPal* (CSV example), that include a *placeholder* into which I can insert the affiliate id when required. In Figure 25 I create a PayPal button for my book `Working with Yahoo! Pipes, No Programming Required`, and I use the (optional) field `Item ID/number` to record the replaceable text `[AFFILIATE_ID]`.

**Figure 25 Create PayPal button with [AFFILIATE_ID]**

Upon completion, the PayPal button creation process offers the following HTML code for me to incorporate in my web page. Note the replaceable text [AFFILIATE_ID], which I have shown bold.

```
<form action="https://www.paypal.com/cgi-bin/webscr" method="post">
<input type="hidden" name="cmd" value="_xclick">
<input type="hidden" name="business"
value="myemailaddress@somewhere.com">
<input type="hidden" name="item_name" value="Working with Yahoo! Pipes,
No Programming Required">
<input type="hidden" name="item_number" value="[AFFILIATE_ID]">
<input type="hidden" name="amount" value="2.75">
<input type="hidden" name="no_shipping" value="0">
<input type="hidden" name="no_note" value="1">
<input type="hidden" name="currency_code" value="GBP">
<input type="hidden" name="lc" value="GB">
<input type="hidden" name="bn" value="PP-BuyNowBF">
<input type="image"
src="https://www.paypal.com/en_GB/i/btn/btn_paynow_SM.gif" border="0"
name="submit" alt="Make payments with PayPal - it's fast, free and
secure!">
<img alt="" border="0"
src="https://www.paypal.com/en_GB/i/scr/pixel.gif" width="1"
height="1">
</form>
```

I insert this HTML into a web page, along with two other buttons I have created plus a heading text that reads [AFFILIATE_NAME] in association with LOTONtech. You can see this affiliate page template in Figure 26 and online at http://www.btinternet.com/~lotontech/pipes/html/Aff iliatePageTemplate.html.

Now we move on to the Pipe design, which you can see in Figure 27. This Pipe uses Text Input modules to take in an Affiliate Name and Affiliate Id as input; it uses a Fetch Page module to read in the affiliate page template from the URL just given; and it uses a Regex module to replace the [AFFILIATE_NAME] and [AFFILIATE_ID] placeholders, in the template page content, with the user-entered values. Finally, a Rename module renames the item.content as description so that the revised HTML will be rendered in the Pipe's RSS output.

**[AFFILIATE_NAME] in association with LOTONtech**

The following books are available now as PDFs:

**Working with Yahoo! Pipes, No Programming Required**                      Pay Now

**Introduction to Microsoft Popfly, No Programming Required**            Pay Now

**Safe Family Computing with Windows Vista**                                    Pay Now

**Figure 26 AffiliatePageTemplate.html**

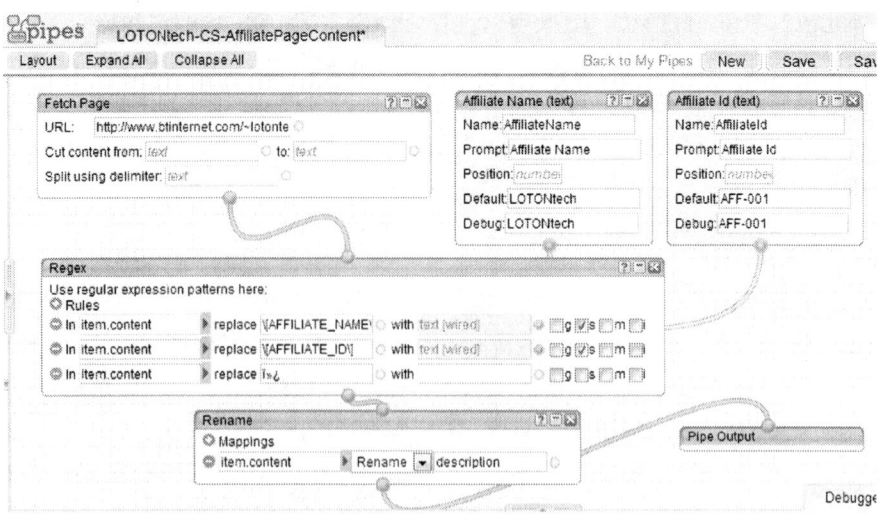

**Figure 27 LOTONtech-CS-AffiliatePageContent**

Note that this Pipe creates affiliate-branded HTML description, containing affiliate-identified PayPal buttons, for any given `Affiliate Name` and `Affiliate Id`. So I could obtain the personalized HTML for a fictional affiliate name `PDFtech` / affiliate id `AFF-002` by visiting this URL:

```
http://pipes.yahoo.com/pipes/pipe.run?AffiliateName=PDFtech&
AffiliateId=AFF-002&_id=Aj5oAVHv3BGHXTiHJphxuA&_render=rss
```

The fictional affiliate `PDFtech` could hyperlink to their storefront content using this URL, but the RSS rendering would be unsatisfactory for potential purchasers. The solution would be for me, or for the affiliate itself, to create a web page that embeds the JSON output of the Pipe as described earlier in *eBay (JSON* in Web Page example). The HTML content of this page would be:

```
<html>

<head>

  <script type="text/javascript">

    function pipeCallback(obj)
```

```
   {
     var x;
     for (x = 0; x < obj.count ; x++)
     {
        var buildstring = "<b><a href=" + obj.value.items[x].link + ">"
+ obj.value.items[x].title + "</a></b>. <span id=desc>" +
obj.value.items[x].description + "</span><br />";

        document.write(buildstring);
        buildstring = null;
     }

     document.write("</div>");
   }

 </script>

</head>

<body>

 <script type="text/javascript"
src="http://pipes.yahoo.com/pipes/pipe.run?AffiliateId=AFF-
002&AffiliateName=PDFtech&_id=Aj5oAVHv3BGHXTiHJphxuA&_render=json&_call
back=pipeCallback">
 </script>

</body>

</html>
```

Assuming that I created this web page on behalf of the affiliate, I could provide them with a link to their unique storefront at:

```
http://www.btinternet.com/~lotontech/pipes/html/PDFtechAffiliat
ePage.html
```

When directed to this link, referred visitors would see Figure 28.

**Figure 28 Affiliate Storefront**

By including the URL of this page as the source of an `<iframe>`, the affiliate could surround this content with any other content they liked – to make it look seamless in their own web site.

## Summary

It should be fairly obvious that you could combine the techniques demonstrated in this chapter, in order to provide your potential customers with a range of buying options. Each item in your catalogue could be displayed along with three links: `Buy from Amazon`, `Pay Now using PayPal`, and `Find it on eBay`.

This idea leads us nicely to the next chapter, in which we use Pipes to perform price comparisons.

# 5 Case Study – Price Comparison

As I write this in early 2008, price comparison web sites seem to be big business – at least in the UK. Every other TV advertisement right now is for *moneysupermarket.com*, *gocompare.com*, *comparethemarket.com*, and many others. These web sites tend to focus on financial products and insurance, but there are other web sites that compare prices of other products – such as *bookfinder4u.com* for book price comparisons.

## Case Study Scenario
In this case study I'm interested in developing Pipes that collect prices for a single item, or type of item, from various sellers. This might be for my own personal use, or to present to others via my own web portal.

The examples demonstrate how this might be applied to books, to credit cards and other financial products, or to items that are sold both on Amazon and on eBay.

## Mashup Implementations
The examples in this section demonstrate how Pipes may be used to combine price information from different web sites, for comparison purposes. They also demonstrate how a Pipe may be used to scrape information from an established price comparison web site.

These examples show how one Pipe can invoke another, either as a sub Pipe or by invoking the second Pipe via its URL.

## ISBN Price Comparison (Sub Pipe Example)

You can access the Pipe(s) developed in this example at:
```
http://pipes.yahoo.com/lotontech/cs_amazon_sellers_by_isbn
http://pipes.yahoo.com/lotontech/cs_barnesandnoble_by_isbn
http://pipes.yahoo.com/lotontech/cs_compare_by_isbn
```

I start with a book example, not only because it's my specialist area but also because books have a unique identifier – the ISBN (International Standard Book Number) – which ensures we really are comparing like with like.

Try searching for 'davinci code' at amazon.com and see how many variants you see in paperback, hardback, illustrated and not. Of course they're all different prices, because in a sense they're different books. Now try typing '0385513755' into the search box, which should take you to the details page for the *Special Illustrated Edition* published by Doubleday in 2004. If I search using the ISBN at other online bookstores, I should see details of exactly the same edition.

An example of the kind of site I'd like to emulate is BookFinder4u at www.bookfinder4u.com. Given a book ISBN, it will produce a table of sellers and prices as shown in Figure 29.

| | Store Name | Availability [?] | Price | Shipping [?] | Total [?] | Condition | Store Rating | |
|---|---|---|---|---|---|---|---|---|
| | Amazon.co.uk Marketplace \<Marketplace\> | In Stock | 0.33 GBP | 2.75 1~4 days | Best Price 3.08 You save 93% | Used | ★★★★☆ 12 reviews | Buy at Amazon.co.uk Marketplace |
| | Abebooks \<Marketplace\> | In Stock | 0.50 GBP | 4.28 7~28 days | 4.78 | Used | ★★★★☆ 57 reviews | Buy at Abebooks |
| | Abebooks .co.uk \<Marketplace\> | In Stock | 0.50 GBP | 4.90 7~28 days | 5.40 | Used | ★★★★☆ 57 reviews | Buy at Abebooks .co.uk |
| | Amazon Marketplace \<Marketplace\> | In Stock | 0.45 GBP | 6.29 3~6 weeks | 6.74 | Used | ★★★★☆ 20 reviews | Buy at Amazon Marketplace |
| | Alibris \<Marketplace\> | In Stock | 1.00 GBP | 6.29 2~4 weeks | 7.29 | Used Coupon | ★★★★☆ 55 reviews | Buy at Alibris |
| | Barnes&Noble BookQuest \<Marketplace\> | In Stock | 1.00 GBP | 6.52 7~23 days | 7.52 | Used | ★★☆☆☆ 4 reviews | Buy at Barnes&Noble BookQuest |
| | Amazon.ca Marketplace \<Marketplace\> | In Stock | 0.81 GBP | 7.70 6~8 weeks | 8.51 | Used | ★★★★★ 1 review | Buy at Amazon.ca Marketplace |
| | Amazon.de Marketplace | In Stock | 4.98 GBP | 4.28 7~21 days | 9.26 | Used | ★★★☆☆ 3 reviews | Buy at Amazon.de |

**Figure 29 BookFinder4u**

In Figure 29 I can see that BookFinder4u sources many of its prices from the Amazon Marketplace, so I too will use that as my first source. I can see a list of *new* available copies of the DaVinci Code Special Illustrated Edition – from Amazon and other Marketplace sellers – by visiting this URL:

```
http://www.amazon.com/gp/offer-listing/0385513755?condition=new
```

Figure 30 shows what this page looks like, and of course I could substitute the ISBN (shown in bold above) with any other ISBN.

I can devise a Pipe that takes an ISBN as input, and which uses the `Fetch Page` module and the `Regex` module (both described in the previous chapter) to parse the page into a feed of separate items representing the separate sellers (including Amazon itself). You can see this Pipe's results in Figure 31, and you can access the Pipe online at `http://pipes.yahoo.com/lotontech/cs_amazon_sellers_by_isbn`.

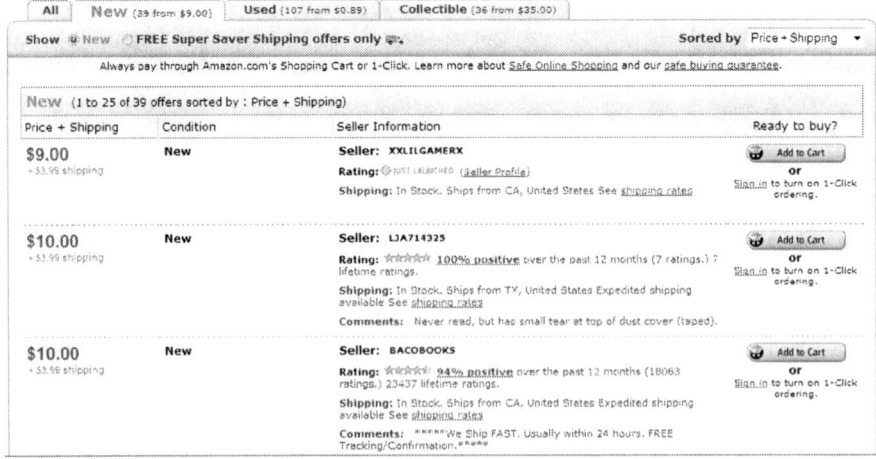

**Figure 30 Amazon Marketplace**

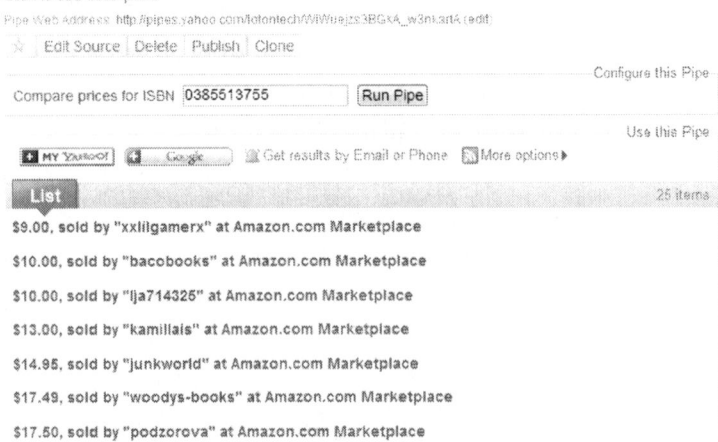

**Figure 31 LOTONtech-CS-AmazonSellersByISBN**

As an alternative to Amazon, I could look up the book's price on Barnes & Noble by following this URL:

```
http://search.barnesandnoble.com/booksearch/isbninquiry.asp?ean=0385513
755
```

Again, I can devise a Pipe that visits the web page and extracts the (single) price as shown in Figure 32. You can access this Pipe at

http://pipes.yahoo.com/lotontech/cs_barnesandnoble_by_isbn.

## LOTONtech-CS-BarnesAndNobleByISBN

*Click to add description*

Pipe Web Address: http://pipes.yahoo.com/lotontech/1a99dcfb7d432cfa6bf10900a6e2c6a8 (edit)

☆ | Edit Source | Delete | Publish | Clone

Configure this Pipe

Get B&N Price for ISBN | 0385513755 | Run Pipe

Use this Pipe

➕ MY YAHOO! | ➕ Google | Get results by Email or Phone | More options ▶

**List** 1 item

$28.00, sold by "Barnes and Noble"

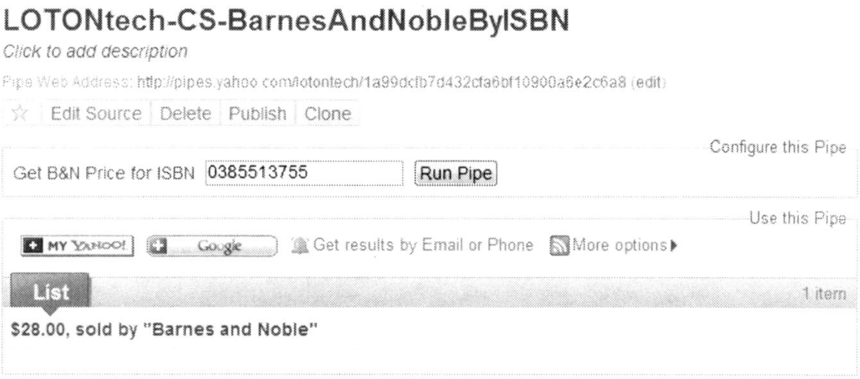

**Figure 32 LOTONtech-CS-BarnesAndNobleByISBN**

What is important here is not how each of these Pipes works internally, but how I can combine their outputs into a single feed – sorted by price.

Figure 33 shows the design of my comparison Pipe; in which I have dragged my two previous Pipes onto the canvas from the My Pipes category of the module library, so that they become sub Pipes. You can always spot a sub Pipe on the canvas by virtue of the [open] link displayed on the module's title bar.

Into each of the sub Pipes I feed the ISBN that I capture using a Text Input module, and I combine the output from both sub Pipes using a Union module.

Although each sub Pipe outputs all necessary information in the feed's title field – for example as $9.00, sold by "xxlilqamerx" at Amazon.com Marketplace – each also outputs the selling price in a separate price field.

In preparation for sorting, I use a `Regex` module to strip out the dollar sign (`$`) from the `price` field of every item in the combined feed. I then use a `Sort` module to sort the combined feed into ascending order of `price`.

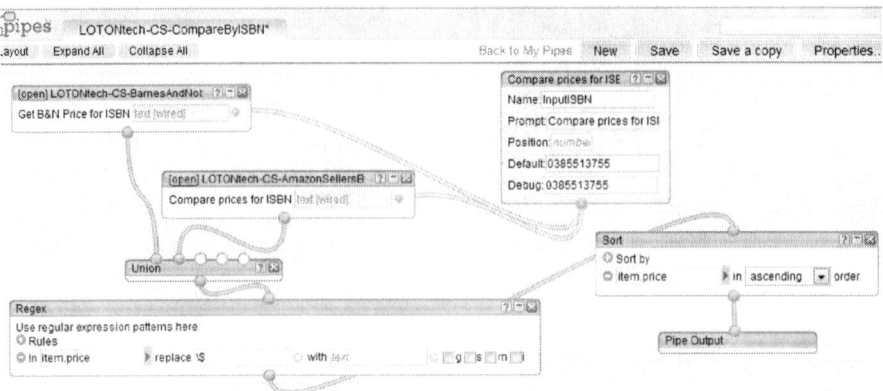

**Figure 33 LOTONtech-CS-CompareByISBN (design)**

When I run the Pipe, the feed output is as shown below. Notice how the entry for 'Barnes and Noble' (shown in bold) has been sorted into the correct price position.

```
$9.00,  sold by "xxlilgamerx" at Amazon.com Marketplace
$10.00, sold by "lja714325" at Amazon.com Marketplace
$10.00, sold by "bacobooks" at Amazon.com Marketplace
$13.00, sold by "kamillais" at Amazon.com Marketplace
$14.95, sold by "junkworld" at Amazon.com Marketplace
$17.49, sold by "woodys-books" at Amazon.com Marketplace
$17.50, sold by "podzorova" at Amazon.com Marketplace
$19.95, sold by "lovethatpaper" at Amazon.com Marketplace
$20.53, sold by "a1books" at Amazon.com Marketplace
$21.51, sold by "international_book_source" at Amazon.com Marketplace
$21.95, sold by "allnewbooks" at Amazon.com Marketplace
$22.71, sold by "--caiman--" at Amazon.com Marketplace
$23.05, sold by "bookrackrh" at Amazon.com Marketplace
$23.10, sold by "fantastic_shopping" at Amazon.com Marketplace
$23.10, sold by "Amazon.com" at Amazon.com Marketplace
$23.87, sold by "pbshopus" at Amazon.com Marketplace
$23.95, sold by "mackbeener" at Amazon.com Marketplace
$24.90, sold by "hwalsh_books_online" at Amazon.com Marketplace
$25.40, sold by "thermite-media" at Amazon.com Marketplace
$25.84, sold by "monster_mart" at Amazon.com Marketplace
$26.06, sold by "mediacrazy" at Amazon.com Marketplace
$26.07, sold by "brandnewgoodsus" at Amazon.com Marketplace
```

```
$26.37, sold by "oddbanana" at Amazon.com Marketplace
$28.00, sold by "gohastings" at Amazon.com Marketplace
$28.00, sold by "Barnes and Noble"
$28.92, sold by "innerselfmarket" at Amazon.com Marketplace
```

## You can access this Pipe at:

```
http://pipes.yahoo.com/lotontech/cs_compare_by_isbn
```

To offer people more buying choices, I could combine the output of additional sub Pipes for other bookstores. And if I was really clever, I could provide hyperlinks for the users to purchase the items.

### ISBN Price Comparison (Invoke Pipe URL example)

You can access the Pipe(s) developed in this example at:
```
http://pipes.yahoo.com/lotontech/cs_compare_by_isbn_2
```

The previous example demonstrated how you can use sub Pipes to invoke previously-developed Pipes from another Pipe; either to factor out reusable sub-functionality, or to make use of other people's Pipes.

Using sub Pipes is a tightly-coupled mechanism, by which I mean that the connection between your main Pipe and its sub Pipe(s) is fixed in the design – unless you change it.

Alternatively, you could invoke other Pipes from within your own Pipe using a more loosely-coupled mechanism. You could invoke Pipes via their URLs by entering their URLs (shown below) into the `Fetch Feed` module.

LOTONtech-CS-BarnesAndNobleByISBN URL:
```
http://pipes.yahoo.com/pipes/pipe.run?
_id=1a99dcfb7d432cfa6bf10900a6e2c6a8&_render=rss&InputISBN=0385513755
```

LOTONtech-CS-AmazonSellersByISBN URL:
```
http://pipes.yahoo.com/pipes/pipe.run?
_id=WiWuejzs3BGkA_w3nkartA&_render=rss&InputISBN=0385513755
```

When I first started using Pipes, I was a big fan of this alternative. It meant that I could easily point my main Pipe at a different sub Pipe by simply changing the URL in the Fetch Feed module; no need to delete the current sub Pipe, no need to drag a new one on to the canvas, and no need and re-make the connections.

Now I'm not such a big fan, and I'll tell you why:-

Figure 34 shows an alternative design for an ISBN price comparison Pipe. From the Union module onwards it's the same as before, but prior to the Union module it's rather more complex since I need to build the URLs incorporating the user-entered ISBN. But that's not the real problem. The real problem is that the combined list does not sort properly.

Do you remember that the Sort module sorts by item.price? Well, item.price is not an RSS field and is therefore not returned by the RSS output feeds of the two sub Pipes; which means that in this design it is not available to the Sort module; which means that the combined output is not sorted as intended.

My attempt to resolve this problem by removing _render=rss from the Pipes' URLs failed, as did my attempt to resolve the problem by replacing it with _render=rss. So in this example, invoking other Pipes via their URLs is not a credible alternative to invoking them as sub Pipes.

Where the technique for invoking a Pipe via its URL really comes into its own, is in integrating with other mashup development environments; a subject that I cover in a later chapter.

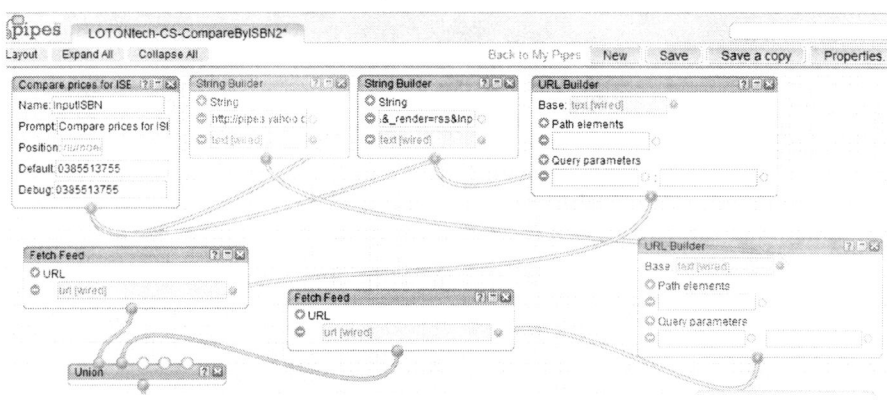

**Figure 34 LOTONtech-CS-CompareByISBN2**

## Credit Card Comparison (JSON and IFrame example)

You can access the Pipe(s) developed in this example at:
`http://pipes.yahoo.com/lotontech/cs_fool_uk`

You can access the Web Page(s) developed in this example at:
`http://www.btinternet.com/~lotontech/pipes/html/FoolCreditCards.html`
`http://www.btinternet.com/~lotontech/pipes/html/LOTONtechFinancePortal.html`

The technique just described in the previous example allows you to offer price comparisons over which you have total control – if you are willing to put some effort into developing the Pipe(s). Alternatively you may wish to act merely as a price comparison portal, offering *views* onto the price comparisons published by other web sites.

Take, for example, the credit card comparison provided by Fool.co.uk at `http://www.fool.co.uk/credit-cards/credit-cards-comparison.aspx`. On this page there is a credit card comparison table (which you might want to present to web site visitors) and lots of surrounding information (which you wouldn't). In a nutshell, you'd like to *scrape* a portion of the web page for presentation in your portal.

We've done some screen scraping in previous examples, using the `Fetch Page` module, and we'll do the same thing again here. This time it's really simple.

In Figure 35, you can see that my Pipe uses a `Fetch Page` module to fetch the credit card comparison page from `http://www.fool.co.uk/credit-cards/credit-cards-comparison.aspx` and cut the HTML content between the `<table>` and `</table>` tags. There is only one table on the page, and it contains all the information I'm interested in. A `Rename` module then renames `item.content` to `description` for display purposes.

In the debugger window, also shown in Figure 35, you can see the resulting HTML table that I intend to display on a web page.

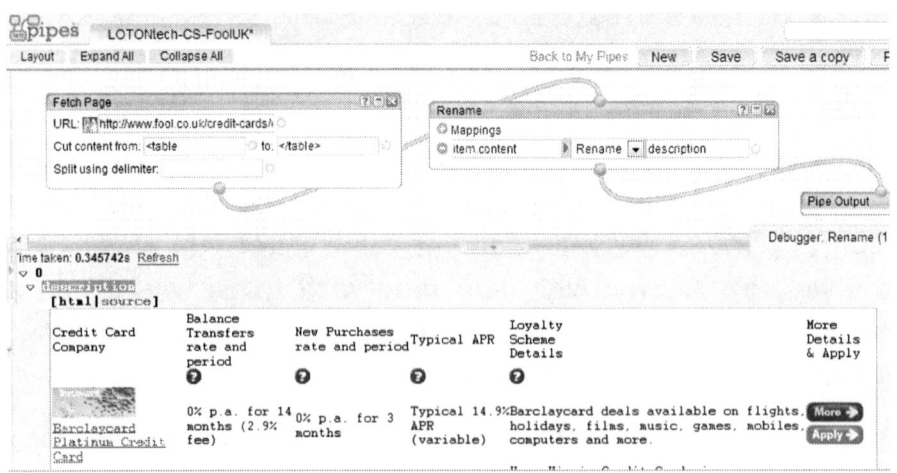

**Figure 35 LOTONtech-CS-FoolUK**

In order to embed the Pipe's output in a web page, I use exactly the same HTML and JavaScript code that I used in the *eBay (JSON in Web Page example)* example of *Chapter 4 Case Study – Selling Online*. Exactly the same, that is, apart from the change of title and Pipe id shown in bold in the following listing.

```html
<html>

<head>

  <script type="text/javascript">

    function pipeCallback(obj)
    {
      document.write("<div><h3>Latest Credit Card Deals from
Fool.co.uk</h3>");
      var x;
      for (x = 0; x < obj.count ; x++)
      {
        var buildstring = "<b><a href=" + obj.value.items[x].link + ">"
+ obj.value.items[x].title + "</a></b>. <span id=desc>" +
obj.value.items[x].description + "</span><br />";

        document.write(buildstring);
        buildstring = null;
      }

      document.write("</div>");
    }

  </script>

</head>

<body style="background-color: #FFFFFF">

  <script type="text/javascript"
src="http://pipes.yahoo.com/pipes/pipe.run?_id=8g2O_VPs3BGSkWSBJphxuA&_
render=json&_callback=pipeCallback">
  </script>

</body>

</html>
```

If I save this listing in a file named `FoolCreditCards.html`, and open it in my browser, I am rewarded with Figure 36. You can access this page for yourself at `http://www.btinternet.com/~lotontech/pipes/html/FoolCred itCards.html`.

In a true *portal* I'd like these results not to occupy the whole page, but to be one component – perhaps amongst many – within a container page. I therefore create a container page named `LOTONtechFinancePortal.html` having the following HTML content:

```
<html>

<head></head>

<body style="background-color: #D5DDFF">

<h1>LOTONtech Finance Portal</h1><br>

<iframe width="800" height="300" src="FoolCreditCards.html"
name="FoolFrame"/>

</body>

</html>
```

When I open this page, as shown in Figure 37, you can see that the containing page has my own title text and background color. The Pipe output is contained wholly within the scrollable inline frame. You can access this page for yourself at `http://www.btinternet.com/~lotontech/pipes/html/LOTONtechFinancePortal.html`.

Latest Credit Card Deals from Fool.co.uk

| Credit Card Company | Balance Transfers rate and period | New Purchases rate and period | Typical APR | Loyalty Scheme Details | More Details & Apply |
|---|---|---|---|---|---|
| Barclaycard Platinum Credit Card | 0% p.a. for 14 months (2.9% fee) | 0% p.a. for 3 months | Typical 14.9% APR (variable) | Barclaycard deals available on flights, holidays, films, music, games, mobiles, computers and more. | More ➜ Apply ➜ |
| money Virgin Credit Card | 0% p.a. for 15 months (2.98% fee) | 0% p.a. for 3 months | Typical 15.9% APR (variable) | Your Virgin Credit Card gives you instant discounts all over the shop. Get money off your holidays, wine, music, DVDs, car insurance... simply by paying with your Virgin Credit Card | More ➜ Apply ➜ |
| egg Egg Credit Card | 0% p.a. until 1st May 2009 (3% fee) | 0% p.a. up to 3 months | Typical 16.9% APR (variable) | Anniversary Offer: 0% for five months on balance transfers made in January 2010 and January 2011 (2.5% fee) | More ➜ Apply ➜ |
| CapitalOne Capital One Platinum Credit Card | 0% p.a. until 1st November 2008 (1.7% fee) | 0% p.a. until 1st November 2008 | Typical 9.9% APR (variable) | No | More ➜ Apply ➜ |
| MBNA Credit Card | 0% pa for 13 Months (2.9% fee) | 0% p.a. until 1st Jun 2008 | Typical 15.9% APR (variable) | No | More ➜ Apply ➜ |

**Figure 36 FoolCreditCards.html in Browser**

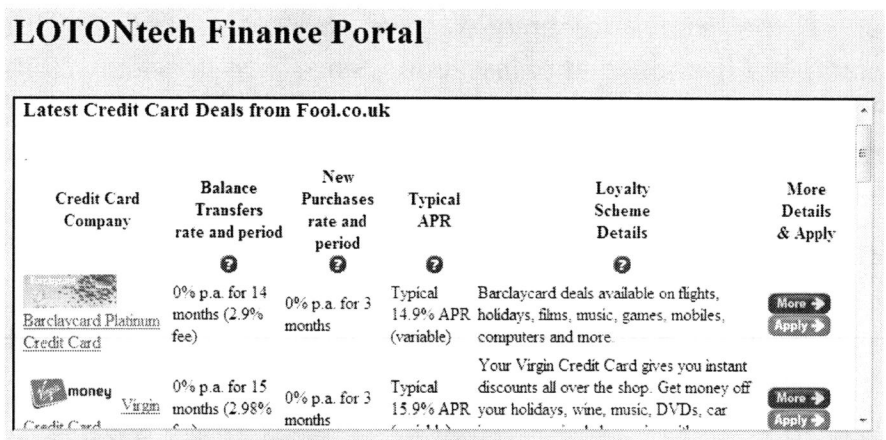

**Figure 37 LOTONtechFinancePortal.html in Browser**

## Amazon / eBay Comparision (Invoke URL example)

You can access the Pipe(s) developed in this example at:
`http://pipes.yahoo.com/lotontech/cs_amazon_ebay_comparison`

Several Pipes published by other Pipe developers have been designed to perform price comparisons across Amazon and eBay. One such example is the Pipe that can be found at `http://pipes.yahoo.com/wristwatchesdealsonline/rolex`, which takes a search term (default 'Rolex Watch'), a min price and max price, an Amazon category (default 'Jewelry'), and a number of results to display.

To save designing our own Pipe for Amazon vs. eBay price comparisons we could:

- Clone the above Pipe and adapt it for our own purposes.

- Or, use this existing Pipe as a sub Pipe in our own Pipe design.

- Or, fetch the feed from this Pipe via its URL and then further process the feed output.

All of the above techniques are applicable, but in this example I'll choose the last one. Since my previous *ISBN Price Comparison (Invoke Pipe URL example)* example did not work out as expected, I thought it would be good to present an 'invoke URL' example that does work out.

If you take a look at this Pipe's RSS feed output at the following URL, you will notice that Amazon results are not distinguished from eBay results (unless you figure out that the eBay results have pictures attached):

```
http://pipes.yahoo.com/wristwatchesdealsonline/rolex?_render=rss&maxPri
ce=8000&minPrice=2000&resultsNo=100&searchInd=Jewelry&textinput1=Rolex+
Watch
```

I'd like to take advantage of this ready-made Pipe, but make the source of each entry more obvious by prefixing the item titles with AMAZON or EBAY as appropriate.

I achieve this objective with the Pipe design shown in Figure 38. First, I use a `Fetch Feed` module to fetch the RSS feed from the Pipe at the URL shown above. Then, I use the `Rename` module to copy the `link` field into a new field named `source`. Next, I use a `Regex` module to replace the link URL in the `source` field with the text AMAZON, if the URL contains the text `amazon.com`; and in the same `Regex` module I replace the link URL in the `source` field with the text EBAY, if the URL contains the text `ebay.com`. Finally, I `Loop` through the feed items, and affix the item `source` field (AMAZON or EBAY) to each item's `title`.

The end result is shown in Figure 39. This output could now be embedded in a web page as an RSS feed, or by utilizing the equivalent JSON output as described previously.

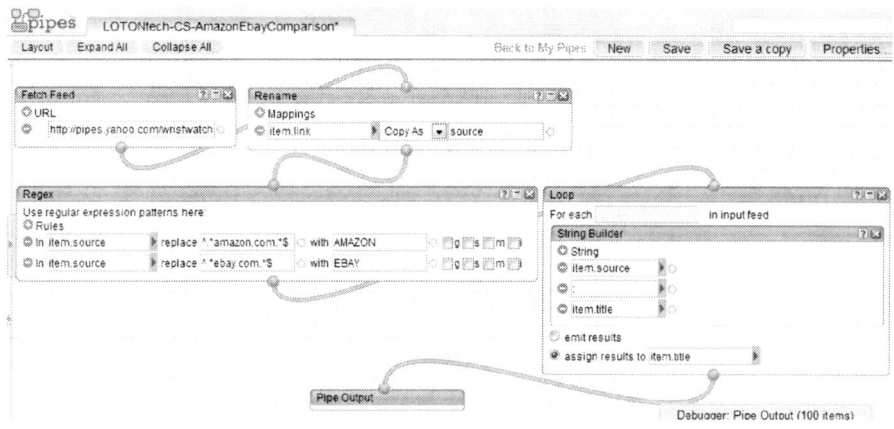

**Figure 38 LOTONtech-CS-AmazonEbayComparison (design)**

AMAZON: Baume & Mercier Riviera Mens Black Dial Stainless Steel Automatic Chronograph Watch 8669 (price: $2,069.99)
Stainless Steel Case and Bracelet, Black Dial, White Roman Numerals, Small Seconds Sub Dial at the 9 o'clock position. Automatic Chronograph Movement, Date at the 3 o'clock Position, Water Resistant to 165 Feet. (Average rating: )

AMAZON: Omega Men's Speedmaster Chronograph Watch #3211.31 (price: $2,050.00)
Silver Dial with Black Sub Dials Chronograph Function Self Winding Automatic Chronometer Movement Caliber: Omega 1164, Power Reserve: 44 Hours Brushed with Polished Steel Case & Bracelet Scratch Resistant Sapphire Crystal 100 Meters / 330 Feet Water Resistant 40mm Case Deployment Buckle...

EBAY: Rolex Ladies 6916 Oyseter Perpetual Diamonds Watch (price: 2299)
US $2,299.00 End Date: Monday Mar-10-2008 12:20:25 PDT Buy It Now for only: US $2,299.00 Buy it now | Add to watch list

EBAY: STAINLESS ROLEX DATE-JUST MENS WATCH MOP DIAMOND DIAL (price: 2299.99)

**Figure 39 LOTONtech-CS-AmazonEbayPriceComparison (running)**

## Summary and Disclaimer

In this chapter I have demonstrated how Pipes could be used to provide price comparison mashups that compare prices within, and between, product-selling web sites. From a technical perspective I have shown how one Pipe can invoke another Pipe via its URL or as a sub Pipe, and I have demonstrated how to screen-scrape information from a web site so as to present it in your own portal.

Be careful about scraping copyrighted information from other organization's web sites and re-publishing it on your own site. Although mashup environments like Yahoo! Pipes implicitly encourage the extraction, processing, and republication of information from web sources, the legal position on this may be uncertain. In this chapter I have described the techniques you may use, but it's up to you to decide how you use them.

# 6 Case Study – Stock Traders 'Cockpit'

The majority of the previous examples in this book have been related to e-commerce; that is, buying and selling stuff online. We'll change tack slightly in this chapter with an example that will be of interest to stock traders / investors. Ok, I admit that there is an element of 'buying and selling' to this too, but this case study is more about information gathering than it is about actually transacting the trades.

## Case Study Scenario

I have a theory that individual stocks are too risky because any company – even the big ones – can go bust, and therefore it's a bad idea to put all your eggs in one basket. Many experts recommend that you diversify to spread your risk, for example by investing in an Index Tracking Fund, but this is unlikely to generate stellar returns – at least in the short term.

So my latest investment theme is *sector investing*, or, more specifically, investing in *sectors in crisis*. As I write this in Q1 2008, it's not difficult to find a sector in crisis – just look at the financial services / banking sector. In fact, you will be able to look at it with the help of this case study.

I'd like to create a web page that shows me (as a chart) how various sectors are performing, with the ability to select any sector and see related new items. If the chart looks bad, and the news looks bad, I might just be tempted!

## Mashup Implementations

In this section I present a series of examples that constitute the solution(s) to the problems presented in the case study scenario.

But first – in Figure 40 I show the 'Trading Cockpit' end result, so that you know what we're aiming for. The cockpit includes two inline frames. On the left: a collection of `Sector Charts` for financial, property, telecoms, retailing, and energy sectors, so that we can see at a glance which sectors are performing badly. On the right: the latest `Sector News` for whichever sector has been selected on the left.

**LOTONtech Trading Cockpit**

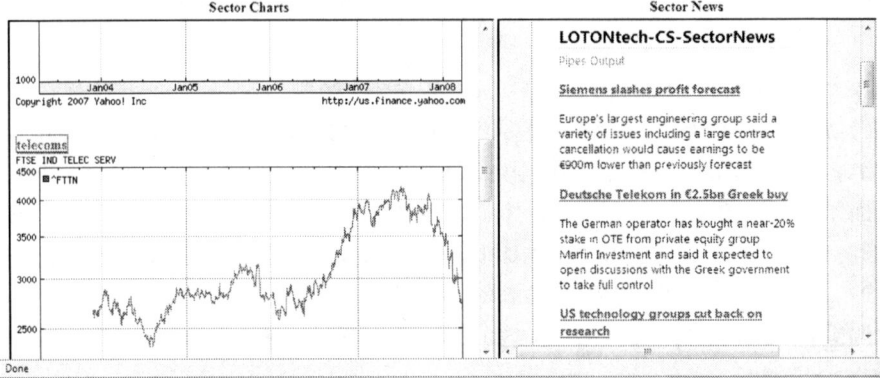

**Figure 40 Trading Cockpit**

What this demonstrates, therefore, is two Pipe mashups displayed on the same web page – with interaction between the two.

You should be able to run this example for yourself at `http://www.btinternet.com/~lotontech/pipes/html/TradingC ockpit.html`.

## Stock Sector Charts (Union example)

You can access the Pipe(s) developed in this example at:
`http://pipes.yahoo.com/lotontech/cs_sector_charts`

The `Sector Charts` frame displayed on the left of the web page (Figure 40) is underpinned by the Pipe shown in Figure 41. It invokes a sub Pipe multiple times, once for each sector that is of interest – namely: `financial`, `property`, `telecoms`, `energy` and (not shown) `retailing`. In each case, `5y` (5 years) is specified as the timeline, but you could change this.

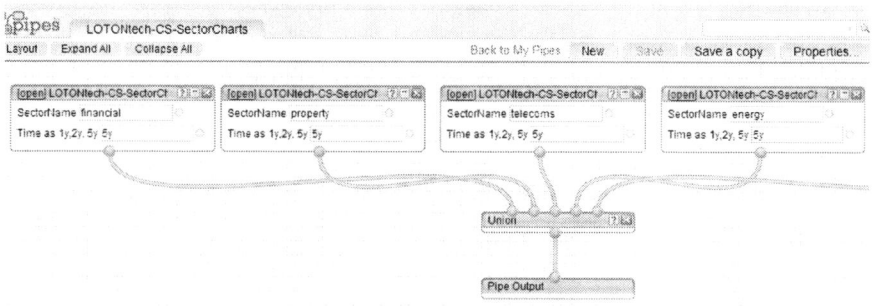

**Figure 41 LOTONtech-CS-SectorCharts**

Each invocation of the sub Pipe returns an RSS feed containing one entry, with the entry's `description` field containing HTML content representing the relevant sector's price chart.

---

A `Union` module is used to concatenate the individual outputs into a single feed, so that all charts appear in the `Sector Charts` frame of the web page shown in Figure 40.

The hard work is done in the sub Pipe, presented next.

### Stock Sector Chart (Fetch Page example)

> You can access the Pipe(s) developed in this example at:
> `http://pipes.yahoo.com/lotontech/cs_sector_chart`

The design of the Sector Chart sub Pipe is shown in Figure 42.

The `URL Builder` module takes in a `Time` in years (as `1y`, `2y`, or `5y`), plus a `SectorName` (converted by the `String Replace` module from `financial` to `^FTBK`, `telecoms` to `^FTTN` etc.), and from these constructs a Yahoo! Finance URL of the form:

`http://uk.finance.yahoo.com/q/bc?z=m&t=`**`5y`**`&s=`**`%5EFTBK`**`&q=l&l=on&c=`

This yields a 5-year price chart for the relevant sector, which you can verify by entering the URL directly in your web browser.

The `Fetch Page` module reads in the web page from the URL and cuts out the surrounding HTML content to retain only the chart. The `Rename` module copies the chart HTML content to the `title`, `link`, and `description` fields, although for the first two fields this will be a temporary measure.

Finally, the `Regex` module cuts out some superfluous HTML content from the `description` field, to retain only the chart image and nothing else. It also replaces the `title` field with the user-supplied `SectorName` and replaces the `link` field with a URL constructed (by the `String Builder` module) from the `SectorName`.

The link is actually the URL, of the form shown next, of another pipe. When the user clicks the link, he or she will be directed to this URL:

```
http://pipes.yahoo.com/pipes/pipe.run?_id=8sEKW4Py3BGklVflBx2yXQ&_rende
r=rss&SectorName=financial
```

Note that this additional Pipe is <u>not invoked</u> when the current Pipe executes, but <u>will be invoked</u> when a user clicks one of the links in the `Sector Charts` frame of Figure 40.

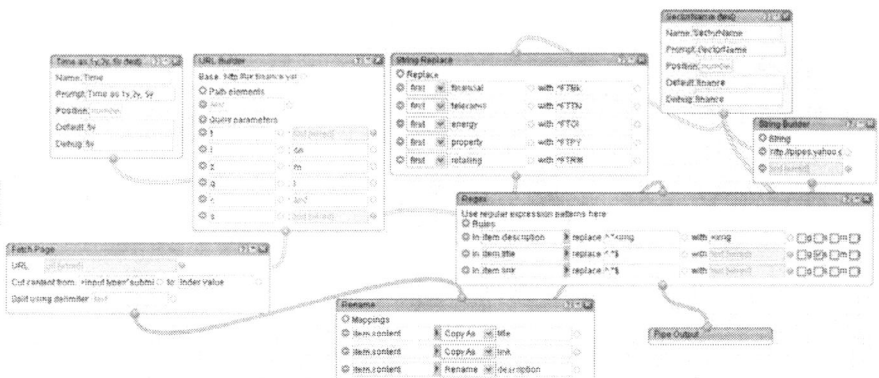

**Figure 42 LOTONtech-CS-SectorChart**

The additional Pipe, described next, is responsible for displaying the sector-related news for whichever sector chart link the user selects.

## Sector News (RSS Feed example)

You can access the Pipe(s) developed in this example at:
http://pipes.yahoo.com/lotontech/cs_sector_news

The design of the Sector News Pipe is shown in Figure 43. It simply accepts `SectorName` as input, builds a URL (shown below) to the sector-related news feed on ft.com, and fetches the RSS feed to output as-is.

```
http://www.ft.com/rss/companies/financial (for 'financial' sector news)
http://www.ft.com/rss/companies/telecoms (for 'telecoms' sector news)
etc.
```

You can visit these URLs yourself to see the news feeds.

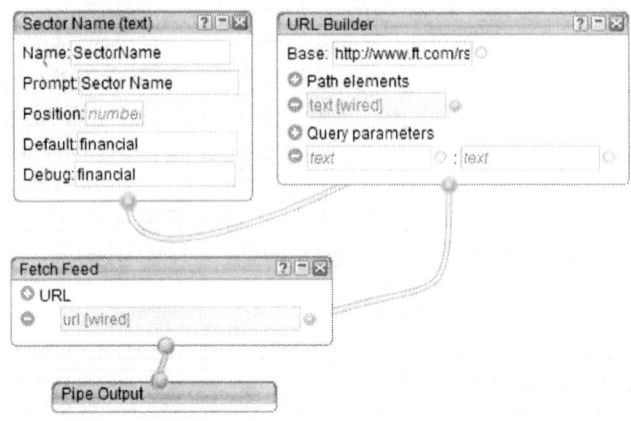

**Figure 43 LOTONtech-CS-SectorNews**

Now that we have the underlying Pipes for this case study, it's time to build them into the 'cockpit' web page.

## Stock Trading 'Cockpit' (Mashups in Page example)

You can access the Web Page(s) developed in this example at:
```
http://www.btinternet.com/~lotontech/pipes/html/SectorCharts.html
http://www.btinternet.com/~lotontech/pipes/html/TradingCockpit.html
```

Actually, we create two web pages in this example. The first page is named `SectorCharts.html` and contains the HTML code shown below. It invokes the Sector Charts Pipe and embeds its JSON output in the page exactly as in earlier JSON examples.

```
<html>
```

```
<head>

  <script type="text/javascript">

    function pipeCallback(obj)
    {
      var x;
      for (x = 0; x < obj.count ; x++)
      {
        var buildstring = "<b><a href=" + obj.value.items[x].link + ">"
+ obj.value.items[x].title + "</a></b><br> <span id=desc>" +
obj.value.items[x].description + "</span><br />";

        document.write(buildstring);
        buildstring = null;
      }

      document.write("</div>");
    }

  </script>

  <base target="newsFrame">

</head>

<body>

  <script type="text/javascript"
src="http://pipes.yahoo.com/pipes/pipe.run?_id=NFZ_rnzy3BG_LlRc6kjTQA&_
render=json&_callback=pipeCallback">
  </script>

</body>

</html>
```

In the above listing I have shown in bold, not only the Pipe URL, but also the HTML tag <base target="newsFrame">. This tag ensures that the default page target is an inline frame named newsFrame, which means that any link on this page has its content display in that frame. In concrete terms, it means that when a user clicks the title of one of this page's sector price charts, the sector news will be displayed in the newsFrame (to the right in Figure 40).

The `newsFrame` itself is not defined in this web page, but in a containing web page named `TradingCockpit.html,` listed below.

```html
<html>

  <head>
  </head>

  <body>
    <h1>LOTONtech Trading Cockpit</h1>
    <table>
      <tr>
        <th>Sector Charts</th>
        <th>Sector News</th>
      </tr>
      <tr>
        <td>
          <iframe    name="chartsFrame"    width="550"    height="375"
src="SectorCharts.html" target="newsFrame"></iframe>
        </td>
        <td>
          <iframe name="newsFrame" width="425" height="375"></iframe>
        </td>
      </tr>
    </table>

  </body>

</html>
```

This HTML listing could not be simpler, really. It arranges two inline frames (`<iframe>`) in a table: the `chartsFrame` to the left and the `newsFrame` to the right. The `chartsFrame` displays our `SectorCharts.html` web page, and the `newsFrame` initially displays nothing at all; but when the user clicks a link in the `chartsFrame`, remember that the content of the link is redirected into the `newsFrame`.

Although the content destined for the `newsFrame` is delivered by one of our Pipes, you will not see any evidence of that Pipe in any of the web pages `SectorCharts.html` or `TradingCockpit.html`. As described in *Stock Sector Chart*

*(Fetch Page example)* above, the links in the left frame are already encoded to invoke the Pipe using URLs like this:

```
http://pipes.yahoo.com/pipes/pipe.run?_id=8sEKW4Py3BGk1VflBx2yXQ&_rende
r=rss&SectorName=financial
```

So, in this case study, we have made our two mashups interact by devising a first Pipe that builds links to invoke a second Pipe; and we have used some HTML code to redirect the output of the second Pipe into another inline frame.

## Summary

In this chapter I have demonstrated how a rudimentary portal could be developed, consisting of a web page that includes two separate Yahoo! Pipes mashups. Separate, yet interacting, such that clicking a link in one mashup refreshes the other mashup to display relevant content.

Although I've presented this case study in terms of *sector investing*, it should be obvious that only a few tweaks would be required in order to support *stock investing* or *index investing*. The charts to the left could be for individual stocks, such as the 30 stocks of the Dow Jones Industrial Average, with related news to the right for a chosen stock. Or, the charts to the left could be for various stock indexes (e.g. DJIA vs. S&P 500 vs. FTSE 100), with related news shown to the right for a chosen index.

# 7 Case Study – Mapping

One of the most popular uses for mashups is to display a set of locations on a map. Those locations might be the venues for you favorite band's upcoming tour, or they might be the locations of apartments-for-rent in your city. These two examples in particular have already been catered for by numerous mashup examples elsewhere.

For my demonstration of a mapping application that uses Pipes, I'll take a more business oriented example.

## Cast Study Scenario

What's the most common reason for displaying a map on a corporate web site? I reckon it is to display the location of one of the company's offices; and I say "one of" because this is often a two-stage process:

- You click a link to see office locations, as a list or addresses, and…

- For any "one of" them you can click a link to see a map of that particular office location.

I'd like to provide a mashup that shows the locations of <u>all</u> my company's offices on a single map. But I don't have sufficient office locations of my own to make this meaningful, so instead I'll use the office locations of another company – John Wiley & Sons – as the basis of this example. I've chosen Wiley simply because I have previously published books with them.

## Case Study Implementation(s)

In this section, I present a series of examples that constitute the solution(s) to the problems presented in the case study scenario.

### Office Locations Pipe (Location Extractor example)

You can access the Pipe(s) developed in this example at:
http://pipes.yahoo.com/lotontech/cs_wiley_locations

You can see a list of Wiley's international office locations by visiting the URL http://eu.wiley.com/WileyCDA/Section/id-301698.html, where you should see a list like this:

**North America**

**John Wiley & Sons, Inc.**
**Corporate Headquarters**
111 River Street
Hoboken, NJ 07030-5774
Telephone. 201.748.6000 Fax. 201.748.6088
Email: info@wiley.com
Web site: www.wiley.com
Contact Us
Directions to Wiley Corporate Headquarters

**Jossey-Bass/Pfeiffer**
989 Market Street
San Francisco, CA 94103-1741
Telephone: 415. 433-1740
Fax: 415.433.0499

**Wiley Publishing, Inc.**
10475 Crosspoint Blvd.
Indianapolis, IN 46256
Telephone: 317.572.3000

**Blackwell Publishing Inc.**
Commerce Place
350 Main Street
Malden, MA 02148
Telephone: 781.388.8200
Fax: 781.388.8210

**Blackwell Publishing Professional**
2121 State Avenue
Ames, IA 50014-8300
Telephone: 515.292.0140
Fax: 515.292.3348

**U.S. Distribution Center**
**John Wiley & Sons, Inc.**
1 Wiley Drive
Somerset, NJ 08875-1272
Telephone: 800.225.5945
Fax: 732.302.2300
Email: custserv@wiley.com

**U.S. Customer Care Operations**
**Trade & Wholesale**
**John Wiley & Sons, Inc.**
1 Wiley Drive
Somerset, NJ 08875
Telephone: 800.225.5945
(Prompt 1)

**Consumer**
**John Wiley & Sons, Inc.**
10475 Crosspoint Blvd.
Indianapolis, IN 46256
Telephone: 800.434.3422
Consumer Technical Support
Telephone: 317.572.3994
(Prompt 2)

**John Wiley & Sons Canada, Ltd.**
5353 Dundas Street West,
Suite 400
Toronto, Ontario M9B 6H8
Canada
Telephone: 416.236.4433
Fax: 416.236.4447
Email: canada@wiley.com

**Canadian Distribution Center and Customer Service John Wiley & Sons Canada, Ltd.**
6045 Freemont Boulevard
Mississauga, Ontario L5R 4J3
Canada
Telephone: (416) 236-4433
Toll Free Telephone: 1-800-567-4797
Fax: (416) 236-4447
Toll Free Fax: 1-800-565-6802
Email: canada@wiley.com
Contact Us

**Europe**

```
Wiley Europe Ltd.
The Atrium
Southern Gate, Chichester
West Sussex PO19 8SQ
England
Telephone: 44.1243.779777
Fax: 44.1243.775878
Email: customer@wiley.co.uk
...
```

I have shortened the list so as to save space in this book, and because in this example I'm only interested in North America locations.

My Pipe design in Figure 44 scrapes information from the given URL using a Fetch Page module. Nothing remarkable there. It then utilizes a Regex module to strip out unwanted content, and a Rename module to copy the retained content into the output feed's title field. Again, nothing remarkable.

What is remarkable, is my use of the Location Extractor module to annotate each item with a y:location sub-element containing that item's latitude and longitude. In a nutshell: it takes an item's title field (such as shown below), figures out the geographical location from the human-readable address, and adds the y:location sub-element required for rendering on a map.

```
title 111 River Street Hoboken, NJ 07030-5774
y:location
   country United States
   lat 40.745529
   lon -74.030327
   quality 50
   state New Jersey
```

The presence of such y:location sub-elements triggers Yahoo! Pipes to render the feed items in the Map tab by

default, as shown in Figure 45. You can always switch to the
`List` tab to see the feed items as a list.

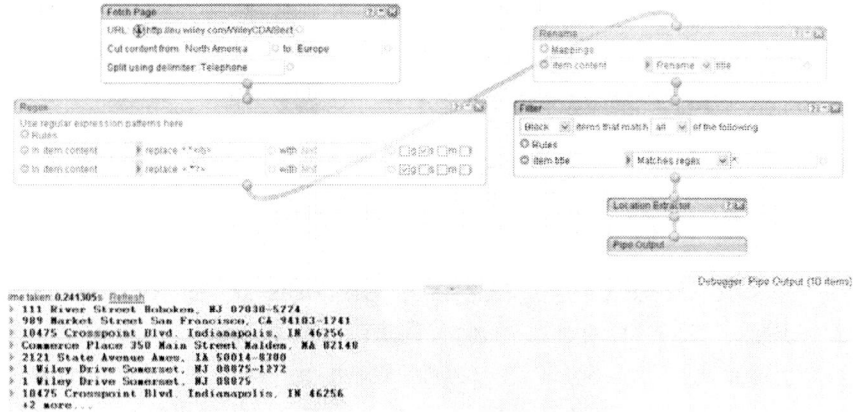

**Figure 44 LOTONtech-CS-WileyLocations (design)**

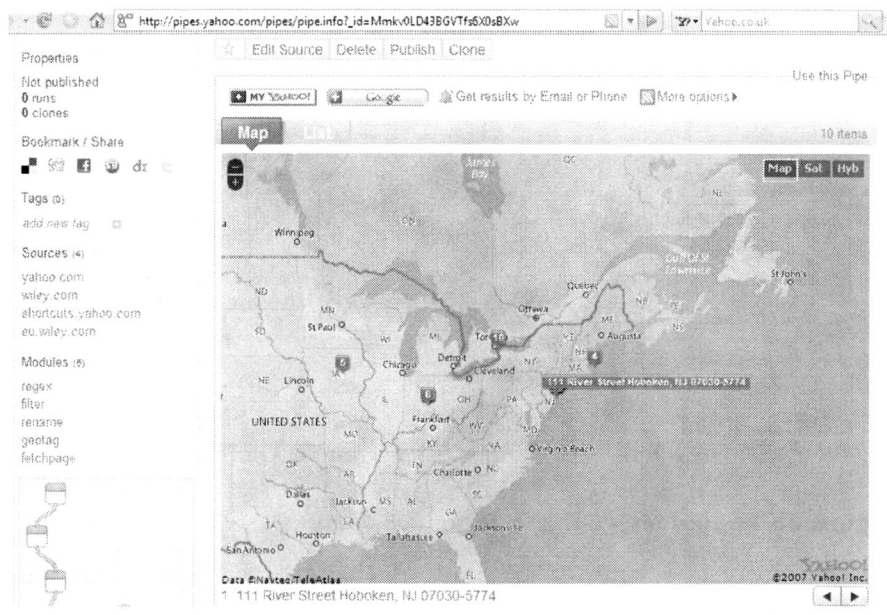

**Figure 45 LOTONtech-CS-WileyLocations (running)**

## Office Locations Map (Google Maps example)

You can access the Web Page(s) developed in this example at:
`http://www.btinternet.com/~lotontech/pipes/html/GoogleMapsPipe.html`

At the time of writing, it was not obvious how such a map could be embedded in one's own web page, but I had a solution.

By selecting the `Get as RSS` option from the Pipe's `More options` menu, I could obtain a URL to the Pipe's RSS output feed, which is:

```
http://pipes.yahoo.com/pipes/pipe.run?_id=Mmkv0LD43BGVTfs6X0sBXw&_rende
r=rss
```

It might not be obvious, but it is possible to enter an RSS feed URL into the search field of Google Maps at `http://www.googlemaps.com`. As long as the feed contains geographical information, i.e. the `y:location` sub-element of my Pipe's items, the locations will be displayed on the Google Map – as shown in Figure 46.

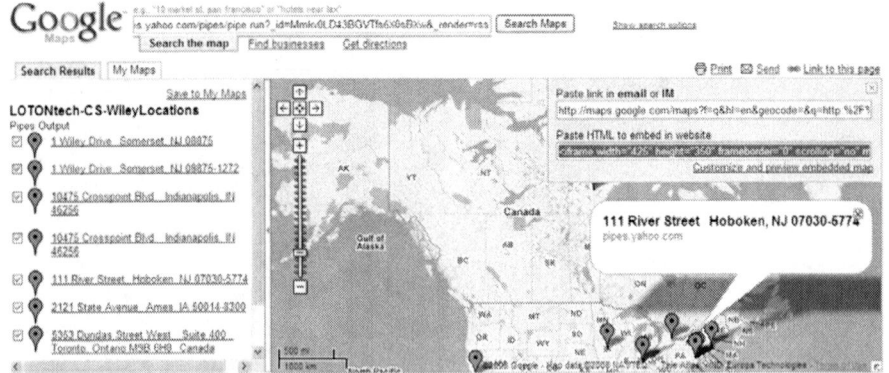

**Figure 46 Google Map using a Pipe RSS feed**

In this figure, I have also clicked the `Link to this page` link, to reveal invitations to…

`Paste link in email or IM:`

```
http://maps.google.com/maps?f=q&hl=en&geocode=&q=http:%2F%2Fpipes.yahoo
.com%2Fpipes%2Fpipe.run%3F_id%3DMmkv0LD43BGVTfs6X0sBXw%26_render%3Drss&
ie=UTF8&z=3
```

`Paste HTML to embed in website:`

```
<iframe width="425" height="350" frameborder="0" scrolling="no"
marginheight="0" marginwidth="0"
src="http://maps.google.com/maps?f=q&amp;hl=en&amp;geocode=&amp;q=http:
%2F%2Fpipes.yahoo.com%2Fpipes%2Fpipe.run%3F_id%3DMmkv0LD43BGVTfs6X0sBXw
%26_render%3Drss&amp;ie=UTF8&amp;ll=50.067115,-
96.73367&amp;spn=24.583229,51.3585&amp;output=embed&amp;s=AARTsJrpMB5oN
H_ekQKAo-KED-1FaKX6zw"></iframe><br /><small><a
href="http://maps.google.com/maps?f=q&amp;hl=en&amp;geocode=&amp;q=http
:%2F%2Fpipes.yahoo.com%2Fpipes%2Fpipe.run%3F_id%3DMmkv0LD43BGVTfs6X0sBX
w%26_render%3Drss&amp;ie=UTF8&amp;ll=50.067115,-
96.73367&amp;spn=24.583229,51.3585&amp;source=embed"
style="color:#0000FF;text-align:left">View Larger Map</a></small>
```

I could now easily create a web page that displays a Google Map showing the office locations provided by my Yahoo! Pipe. In fact, I have, and you can see the result at `http://www.btinternet.com/~lotontech/pipes/html/GoogleMapsPipe.html`.

## Office Locations Map (Get as a Badge example)

You can access the Web Page(s) developed in this example at:
`http://www.btinternet.com/~lotontech/pipes/html/OfficeLocations.html`

As soon as I had written up the Google Maps example above, I noticed that the Yahoo! Pipe's team had introduced an additional facility that considerably simplifies the inclusion of a Pipes-generated map on a web page.

In Figure 47 you should just about be able to see the Get as a Badge link, which launches the pop-up Get this Yahoo! Pipes Badge window also shown in the figure. You are offered various destinations for the badge, which at the time of writing are TypePad, Blogger, WordPress, iGoogle and Embed (in your own web page). By way of demonstration, I chose the iGoogle option so that you can see the map included as a badge on my iGoogle page in Figure 48.

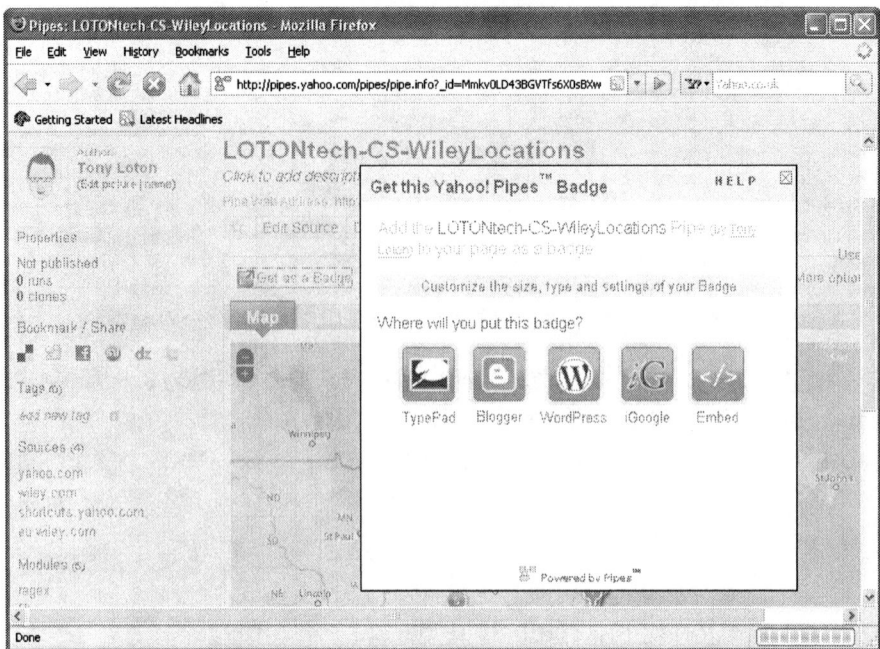

**Figure 47 Get as a Badge**

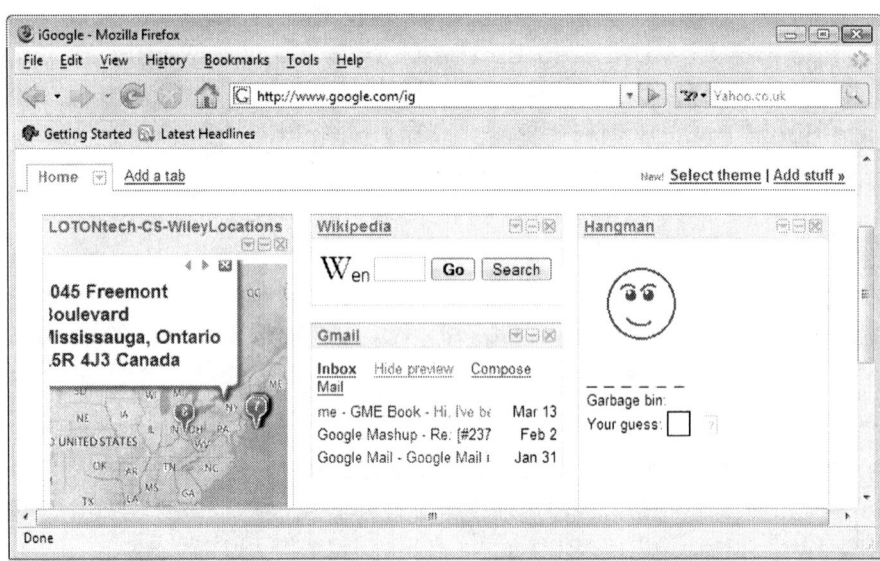

**Figure 48 Yahoo! Pipes Badge on iGoogle**

Choosing the `Embed` option, instead, reveals the following JavaScript code that may be included in a web page:

```
<script
src="http://pipes.yahoo.com/js/mapbadge.js">{"pipe_id":"Mmkv0LD43BGVTfs
6X0sBXw","_btype":"map"}</script>
```

In the listing below I have created the simplest possible web page (HTML) code that includes the script.

```
<html>

<head>
</head>

<body>

<h1>Wiley Office Locations</h1>

<script
src="http://pipes.yahoo.com/js/mapbadge.js">{"pipe_id":"Mmkv0LD43BGVTfs
6X0sBXw","_btype":"map"}</script>

</body>

</html>
```

Saving this listing as file `OfficeLocations.html`, and running it, results in Figure 49.

## Wiley Office Locations

**Figure 49 Yahoo! Pipes Badge Embedded in Web Page**

Whenever you use the `Get as a Badge` option, you can click a link (shown in Figure 47) to `Customize the size, type` and settings of your Badge – which does as the name suggests. Particularly interesting is the ability to change the type of a badge, from a Map to a List. Not only does this mean that a badge could display the set of *office locations* as a list, but also that we could display *any* Pipe-generated feed in the form of a badge; including feeds that contain rich HTML content in their description fields.

Let's digress from mapping applications then, to consider what would happen if I converted the output of my LOTONtech-CS-SectorCharts Pipe (from *Chapter 6 Case Study – Stock Traders 'Cockpit'*) into a badge. Figure 50 shows that the output does display correctly as a badge, and – in case you're wondering – the links to related news stories do work.

The Get as a Badge option therefore provides a third technique for embedding Pipe output in a web page, in addition to the <iframe> and JSON techniques demonstrated in earlier chapters.

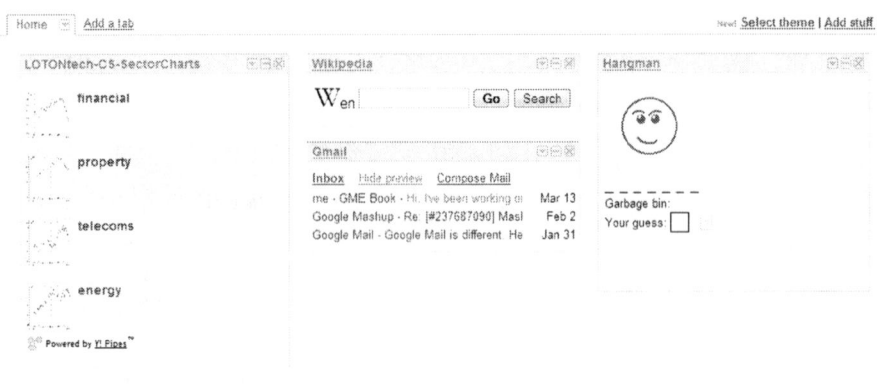

**Figure 50 LOTONtech-CS-SectorCharts as a Badge**

## Summary

In this chapter we have looked into some of the possibilities for creating a Pipe that includes geographical information to be displayed in the form of a map. We took the sample Pipe's output as an input to Google Maps, and also showed how the Pipe's map output could be rendered within a web page using the `Get as a Badge` option.

The specific example in this chapter presented a set of *office* locations on a map. Another popular use for mapping is to show the locations of an organization's customers. In almost every company that I have worked, one wall of the boardroom or sales office has featured a map of the UK or Europe with pinpoints indicating the locations of our customers – often in relation to the locations of our offices.

# 8 Case Study – Mashup Integration

In *Chapter 6 Case Study – Stock Traders 'Cockpit'* we investigated one possible way to make two mashups – both of them Pipes – interact on a single web page. This leads us nicely to the subject presented in this chapter, which is to look at how our Yahoo! Pipes could be made to interact with mashups developed using other mashup development environments.

Yahoo! Pipes is not the only mashup development environment. The two significant competing environments are Microsoft Popfly (http://www.popfly.com) and the Google Mashup Editor (http://googlemashups.com), but in this chapter I aim to show how they may in fact be complementary rather than competitive. Each has its own unique advantages; either in terms of the kinds of mashups you can create, or in the ease-of-use of its development environment. Popfly lends itself to visually appealing interactive mashups, whereas Pipes is ideal for backend processing of RSS feeds. Google Mashup Editor (GME) potentially ticks both of these boxes, but is fundamentally a code editor rather than a graphical development environment.

Aside from the attractions of any one environment, you should also consider the potential audience for your mashup creations. Each environment provides a facility to *publish* your mashup(s) for all to see; so by fronting your Yahoo! Pipe with a GME mashup you could double the size of your audience, and by fronting your Popfly mashup with a Yahoo! Pipe you could do the same.

## Case Study Scenario

In this case study I'll present ideas for fronting a mashup developed in one environment with a mashup developed in another environment: firstly, to widen the potential audience by providing various published access channels to your core fun functionality, and secondly to provide added-value functionality on top of an existing mashup – yours, or someone else's – that has been developed in another environment.

With the three mashup development environments there are six possible permutations as follows, the last two of which I shall ignore since they do not involve Yahoo! Pipes.

- **Popfly to Pipes**

- **Pipes to Popfly**

- **GME to Pipes**

- **Pipes to GME**

- Popfly to GME

- GME to Popfly

## Mashup Implementations

The following implementations will show you what might be achieved by combining mashup technologies, but will not teach you how to develop mashups using Microsoft Popfly nor Google Mashup Editor. If you've dabbled with the other environments – as many Pipes users have – then you'll be able to dive in and have a go. If the other environments are completely new to you, take these examples as inspiration.

Once you are sufficiently inspired, you can learn more from the following books available at `http://www.lotontech.com/it_books.htm`:

- Introduction to Microsoft Popfly, No Programming Required; ISBN 0955676436.

- Creating Google Mashups with the Google Mashup Editor; ISBN 0955676452.

## Sector News and Charts (Popfly to Pipes example)

You can access the Pipe(s) used by this example at:
`http://pipes.yahoo.com/lotontech/cs_sector_news`
You can access the Popfly Mashup developed in this example at:
`http://www.popfly.com/users/LOTONtech/LOTONtech-CS-SectorNews`

Suppose I want to create a Popfly mashup that fronts my Sector News Pipe from the *Sector News (RSS Feed example)* section of *Chapter 6 Case Study – Stock Traders 'Cockpit'*. I might want to do this because I'm not happy with my browsers default rendering of RSS feeds, or so that I can install this functionality as a gadget on my Windows Vista desktop, or simply to make my mashup available to the Popfly community.

I could create the simple three-block Popfly mashup shown in Figure 51. The User Input block prompts for a sector name using a drop-down list, the Text Helper block appends the sector name to my Pipe URL, and the RSS with Comments block displays my Pipe's RSS output feed.

Figure 52 shows the result of executing this Popfly mashup. Compared with my original Pipe mashup, it is self-contained – the single Popfly mashup prompts for the user input and displays the results; no need for a separate HTML form.

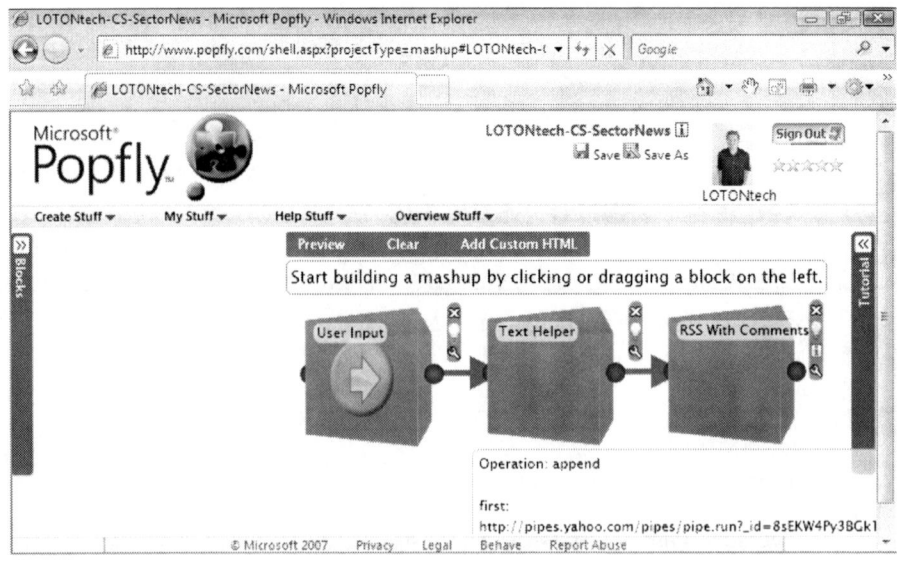

**Figure 51 LOTONtech-CS-SectorNews (Popfly design)**

**Figure 52 LOTONtech-CS-SectorNews (Popfly, running)**

With just a few button clicks on the Popfly web site, I – or anyone else – can download the mashup as a Windows Vista Sidebar Gadget as shown on the right of Figure 53.

Figure 53 also shows the design of a second Popfly mashup, which fronts my Sector Charts Pipe from *Chapter 6 Case Study – Stock Traders 'Cockpit'*. Since there are no user inputs in this case, all I need is a Popfly RSS with Comments block to invoke my Pipe. And I could easily embed this Popfly mashup (which displays the charts supplied by the Pipe) in a web page by using this HTML tag:

```
<iframe style='width:100%; height:100%;'
src='http://www.popfly.com/users/LOTONtech/LOTONtech-CS-
SectorCharts.content' frameborder='no'
allowtransparency='true'></iframe>
```

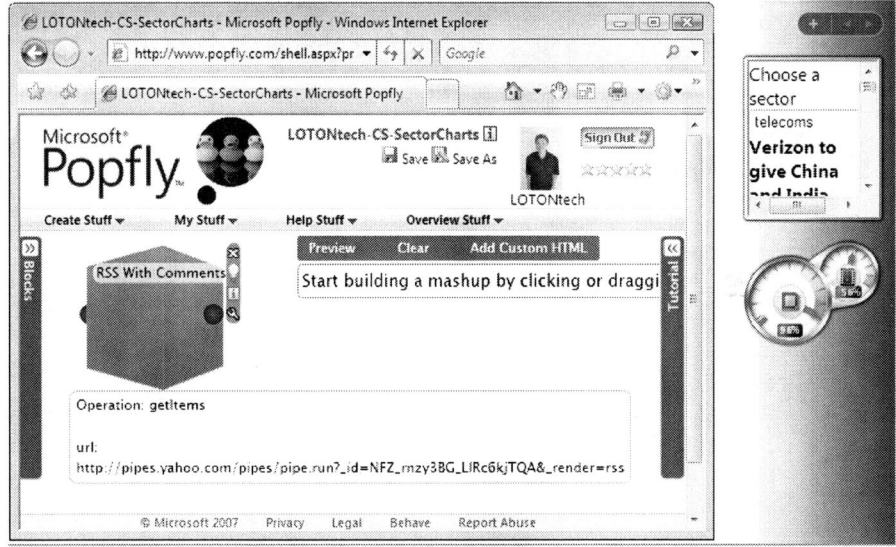

**Figure 53 LOTONtech-CS-SectorNews (design) + Sidebar Gadget**

## MSN Shopping (Pipes to Popfly example)

You can access the Pipe(s) developed in this example at:
http://pipes.yahoo.com/lotontech/cs_msn_shopping

Invoking a Popfly mashup from a Yahoo! Pipe, and capturing its output, is not so straightforward because Popfly mashups do not emit feeds in the way that Yahoo! Pipes do. However, it is possible to design a Yahoo! Pipe that provides a hyperlink to a Popfly mashup, and which passes in some information as a URL parameter.

Consider the Popfly mashup design shown in Figure 54. The `UserInputV2` block gets the `symbol` parameter from the invocation URL and performs a search on `MSN Shopping` using that parameter value. So if I enter the following URL into my web browser, the result will be as shown in Figure 55.

```
http://www.popfly.com/users/LOTONtech/QueryParameterMSNShopping.content
?symbol=phone
```

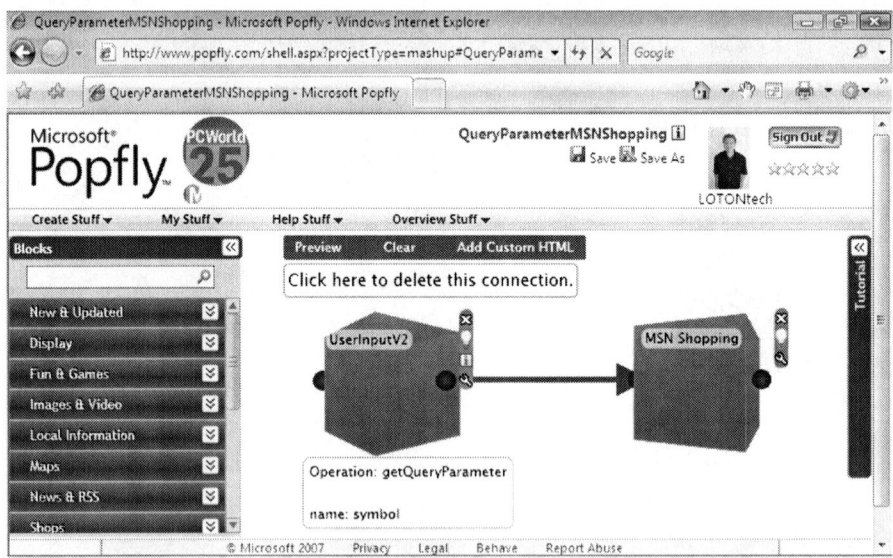

**Figure 54 MSN Shopping Popfly Mashup (design)**

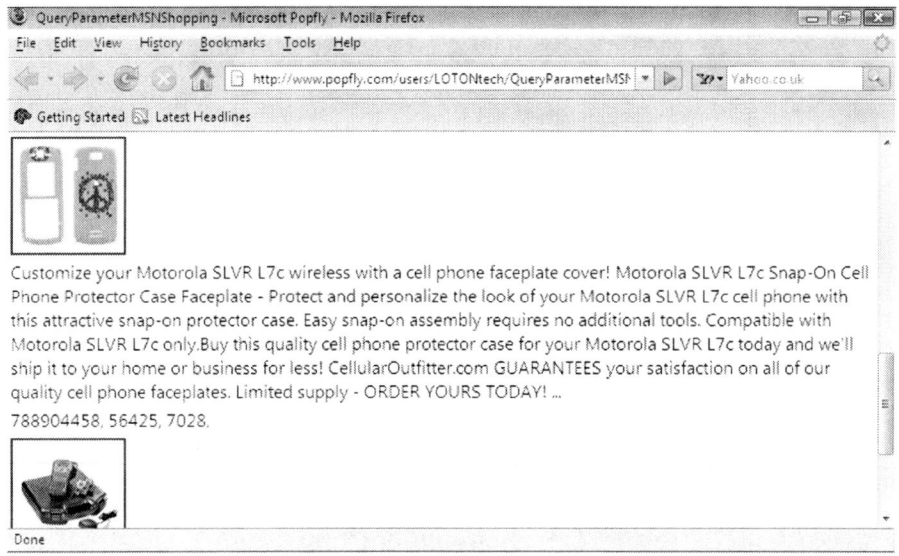

**Figure 55 MSN Shopping Popfly Mashup (running)**

A Yahoo! Pipe to front this Popfly mashup would simply build the invocation URL incorporating a user input, and present this as output in the form of a hyperlink. Figure 56 shows the Pipe design, and Figure 57 shows the Pipe in action. Clicking the link labeled `Click to search for 'phone' on MSN Shopping via Popfly` would take me straight to Figure 55.

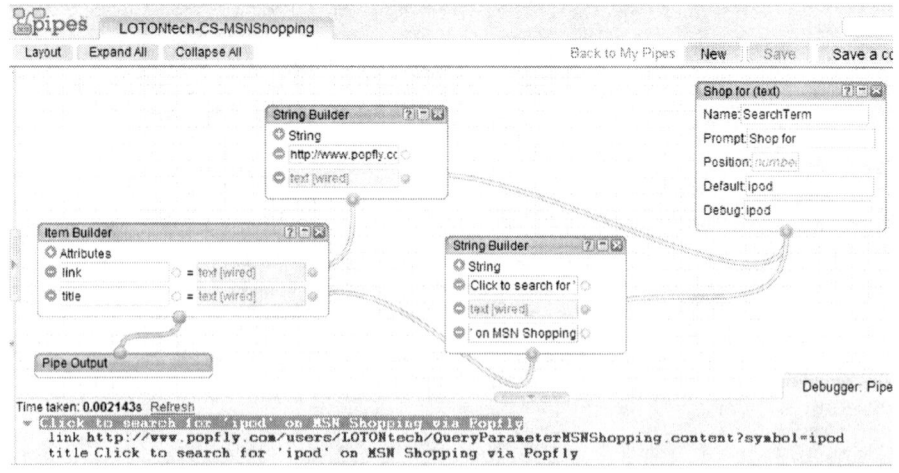

**Figure 56 LOTONtech-CS-MSNShopping (Pipe design)**

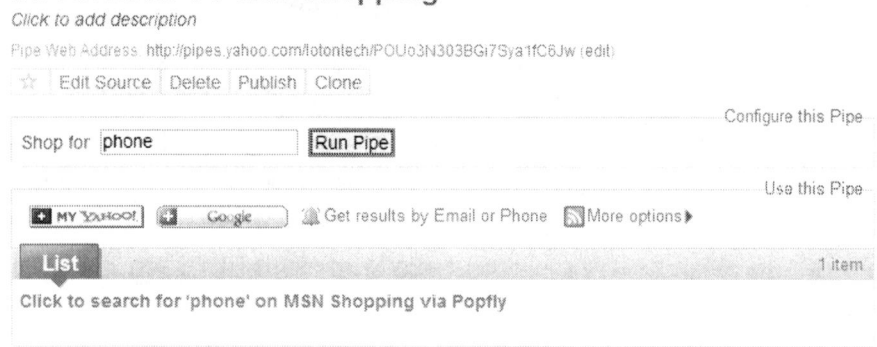

**Figure 57 LOTONtech-CS-MSNShopping (Pipe running)**

The output from this Popfly-fronting Pipe could be embedded in a web page using its JSON or RSS output, and a HTML form could be used to prompt the user for a search term – as in the *Download Links (HTML Form example)* section of *Chapter 4 Case Study – Selling Online*.

Remember that the output will be merely a hyperlink, which, when clicked, will take the user to the page for the Popfly mashup as shown in Figure 55.

## Download Links (GME to Pipes example)

> You can access the Pipe(s) used by this example at:
> `http://pipes.yahoo.com/lotontech/cs_download_links`
> You can access the Google Mashup developed in this example at:
> `http://lotontechdownloads.googlemashups.com/`

In *Chapter 4 Case Study – Selling Online* I devised a Pipe that provides download links for any of my customers, based on the customer's user name. By using the Yahoo! Pipes Get as RSS option, I can determine a URL that provides an RSS feed of download links for any given user. Like this:

```
http://pipes.yahoo.com/pipes/pipe.run?
_id=eL0p1Znu3BGk_Qb1y6ky6g&_render=rss&Username=beckham
```

Now, I'm not very happy with the way web browsers render this RSS list; I don't think that it looks very professional. But, I know that I can use the GME to code up a mashup which:

- takes the RSS feed as input, and

- lets me control exactly how it is rendered

The first step is for me to analyze the source RSS feed in the GME Feed Browser (Figure 58) so as to determine the unique GPath addresses of the various elements of the feed. In the figure I have clicked the download hyperlink URL for the book 'Introduction to Microsoft Popfly' to reveal its GPath, which is: `atom:link[@rel='alternate']/@href`

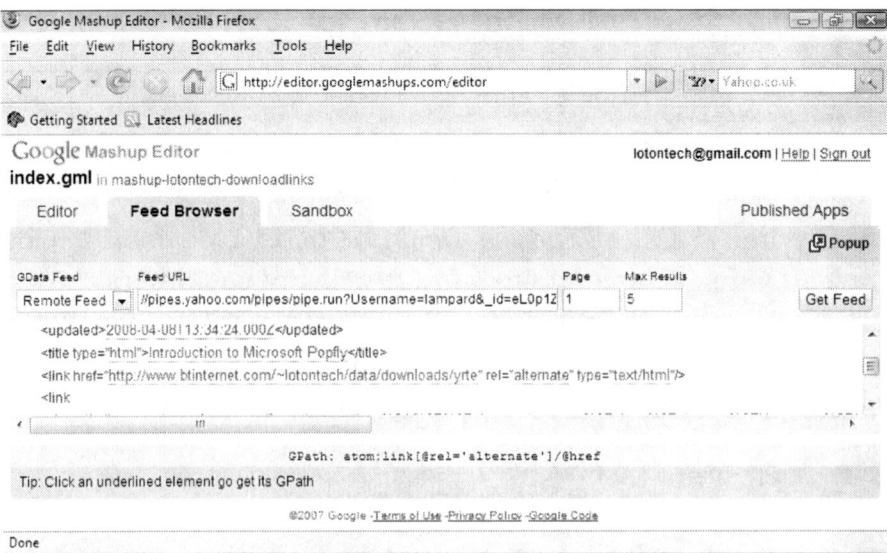

**Figure 58 GME Feed Browser**

Next, I enter the code that follows into the GME's Editor tab. It's not my intention to teach the GME here; so I offer the code for you to study if you wish, or for you to take merely as evidence that it does indeed invoke my Pipe.

```
<gm:page title="LOTONtech-CS-DownloadLinks" authenticate="false">

  <table>
    <tr>
      <td>
        <form name="userNameForm" onSubmit="return
getDownloadLinks();">
          Enter your username:
          <input name="userName" type="text"/>
          <input type="button" value="View Downloads"
onClick="getDownloadLinks();"/>
        </form>
      </td>
    </tr>
    <tr><td><b>Download links...</b></td></tr>
    <tr>
      <td>
        <gm:list id="downloadLinksList"
template="downloadLinksTemplate"
data="http://pipes.yahoo.com/pipes/pipe.run?_id=eL0p1Znu3BGk_Qb1y6ky6g&
_render=rss"/>
      </td>
```

```
    </tr>
  </table>

  <gm:template id="downloadLinksTemplate">
    <table class="gray-theme">
      <tr repeat="true">
        <td valign="top">
          <gm:link label="Download"
ref="atom:link[@rel='alternate']/@href"/>
        </td>
        <td valign="top">
          <gm:text ref="atom:title" width="54" height="41"/>
        </td>
      </tr>
    </table>
  </gm:template>

  <script>
    function getDownloadLinks()
    {
      var userName = document.userNameForm.userName.value;
      if(userName!=null && userName!="")
      {
        var downloadLinksList =
google.mashups.getObjectById('downloadLinksList');
        var url =
'http://pipes.yahoo.com/pipes/pipe.run?_id=eL0p1Znu3BGk_Qb1y6ky6g&_rend
er=rss&Username='+userName.toString();
downloadLinksList.setData(url);
      }
      else
      {
        alert('Enter a user name');
      }
      return false;
    }
  </script>

</gm:page>
```

The end result is the Google Mashup shown in Figure 59. As in the original example of *Chapter 4 Case Study – Selling Online*, it prompts for a user name as input; but this time without requiring HTML code in a separate web page to capture the input. The resulting download links are presented in a list that has better styling than the browser-rendered RSS list of the original example.

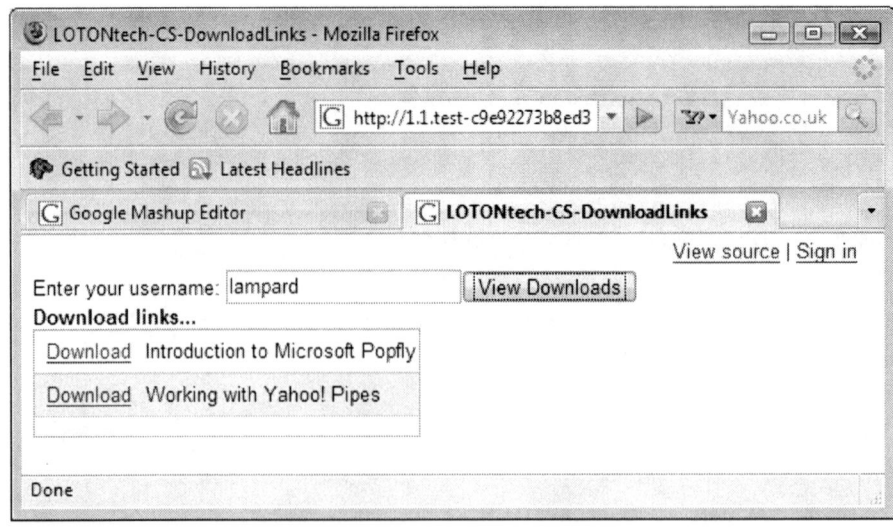

**Figure 59 Download Links Google Mashup**

## Reader Comments (Pipes to GME example)

You can access the Pipe(s) developed in this example at:
`http://pipes.yahoo.com/lotontech/cs_book_comments`
You can access the Google Mashup used by this example at:
`http://lotontechbookcomments.googlemashups.com/`

In this example we'll take a slightly different approach from that taken in the other examples. Rather than invoking a GME application from a Yahoo! Pipe, which should be possible, we'll read a GME application's feed from within a Pipe.

This example is particularly interesting because GME applications can do something that Yahoo! Pipes cannot – that is, they can persist data in a feed. The GME mashup application shown in Figure 60 does just that. It allows any visitor with a Google account to enter a star rating and a comment for any of the books that I have written.

The following tag used within the GME code indicates that the data will be stored in a special feed `${app}/comments`.

```
<gm:list data="${app}/comments" template="commentsTemplate" />
```

It turns out that this feed is also available outside of the GME application, at the following URL; providing I have set the appropriate permissions in the GME application's *publish settings*.

```
http://lotontechbookcomments.googlemashups.com/feeds/app/comments
```

Directing my web browser to this URL yields the XML content shown in Figure 61.

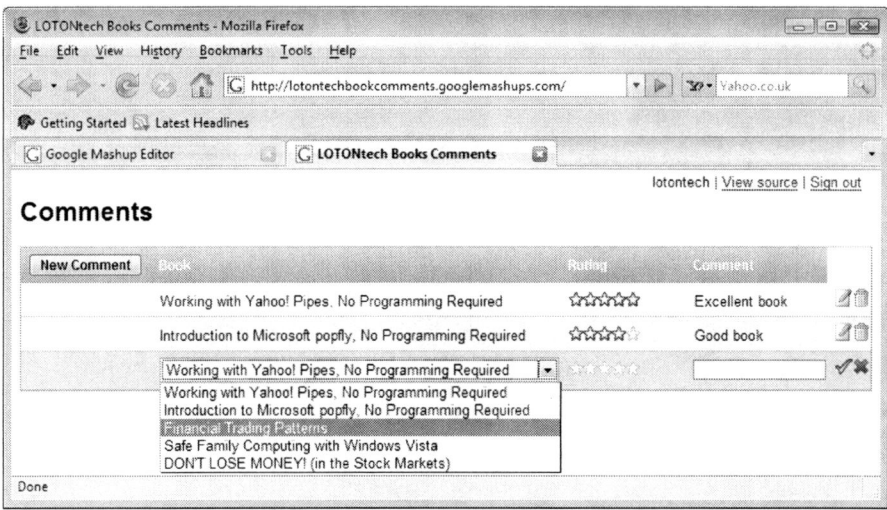

**Figure 60 LOTONtech Books Comments GME Application**

```
- <entry>
  - <id>
      http://lotontechbookcomments.googlemashups.com/feeds/app/comments/1
    </id>
    <published>2008-03-19T13:12:00.465Z</published>
    <updated>2008-03-19T13:12:00.465Z</updated>
    <link rel="self" type="application/atom+xml"
    href="http://lotontechbookcomments.googlemashups.com/feeds/app/comments/1"/>
    <link rel="edit" type="application/atom+xml"
    href="http://lotontechbookcomments.googlemashups.com/feeds/app/comments/1/0"/>
    <gd:book>978-0-9556764-4-4</gd:book>
    <gd:bookRating min="1" max="5" value="5"/>
    <gd:comment>Excellent book</gd:comment>
  </entry>
- <entry>
  - <id>
      http://lotontechbookcomments.googlemashups.com/feeds/app/comments/2
```

**Figure 61 LOTONtech Books ${app}/comments Feed**

Yahoo! Pipes provides a `Fetch Data` module that takes such XML content and "tries to extract a list of elements using the provided path parameter". My Pipe design in Figure 62 directs a `Fetch Feed` module to the GME feed URL and instructs it to extract a list of elements from path `entry`. You can see the content of one such `entry` element in the debugger window at the foot of Figure 62. The list of extracted `entry` elements is emitted from the `Fetch Data` module as a list of Pipes `items`.

After fetching the data, the Pipe renames the `item.gd:book` field of each item as `title` – so that this field (the book's ISBN) becomes the title of an element in the Pipe's output feed.

Finally, the Pipe uses a `Loop` module to iterate through each entry, and within the loop a `String Builder` module combines the `item.gd:bookRating` and `item.gd:comments` fields into a string of the form:

5 stars, **Excellent book**

The final output from the Pipe is shown in Figure 63.

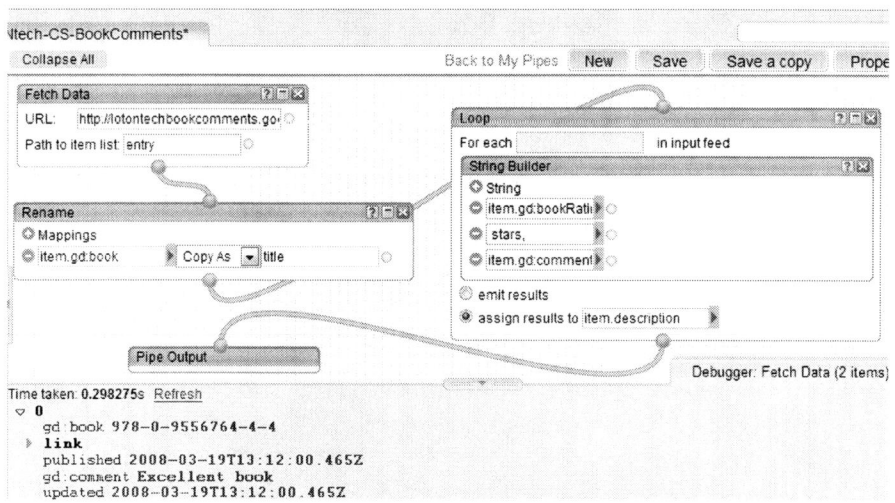

**Figure 62 LOTONtech-CS-BookComments (design)**

## LOTONtech-CS-BookComments

*Click to add description*

Pipe Web Address: http://pipes.yahoo.com/lotontech/1L6AKbf13BG__47D91vC6Jw (edit)

☆ | Edit Source | Delete | Publish | Clone

Use this Pipe

[+] MY YAHOO!   [+] Google   📧 Get results by Email or Phone   📶More options ▶

**List**                                                    2 items

978-0-9556764-4-4
5 stars, Excellent book

978-0-9556764-3-7
4 stars, Good book

**Figure 63 LOTONtech-CS-BookComments (output)**

Consider what we have achieved in this example: we have used a Pipe to read in a data feed that was written by a GME application.

## Summary

This chapter demonstrated how Yahoo! Pipes may be combined with other mashup technologies, such as Microsoft Popfly and Google Mashup Editor – for ever more innovative mashup solutions available to a wider audience.

It concludes the set of case studies presented in this book, and now it's up to you to develop my ideas further to achieve your own mashup objectives. Happy Mashing!

# Also by This Author

Tony Loton's IT books published by LOTON*tech* are available at http://www.lotontech.com/computing.

*Professional Visual Studio 2005 Team System (published by Wrox)*
*Professional UML with Visual Studio .NET (published by Wrox)*
*Web Content Mining with Java (published by Wiley)*

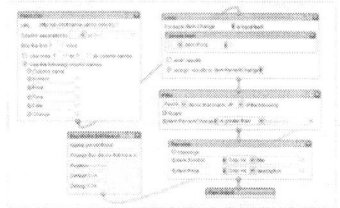

**ISBN-13:** 978-0-9556764-4-4
**ISBN-10:** 0955676444

**Working with Yahoo! Pipes, No Programming Required**

Yahoo! Pipes is a powerful composition tool to aggregate, manipulate, and mashup content from around the web. In this book you will learn how to:

\* Create Pipes by connecting modules together graphically; no programming required.

\* Publish your Pipes for the benefit of others.

\* Discover already-published Pipes.

\* Embed Pipe results in your own web pages.

\* Combine Yahoo! Pipes with Microsoft Popfly to create more innovative mashups.

Many of the chapters conclude with an Exercise for the Reader, which helps you discover more "hands on". And don't worry, the answers are given too!

# Tony Loton

**ISBN-13:** 978-0-95567-643-7
**ISBN-10:** 0955676436

**ISBN-13:** 978-0-9556764-5-1
**ISBN-10:** 0955676452

## Introduction to Microsoft Popfly, No Programming Required

This book introduces Popfly and shows how you can use it to:

* Create web content mashups by connecting predefined building blocks on a design surface; no programming required.

* Create a Popfly hosted web page incorporating one or more mashups.

* Include mashups in your social network profiles, as sidebar gadgets on your Windows Vista desktop, and more.

* Make Popfly friends, share content with them, and rate their projects.

* Use Popfly Explorer to share Visual Studio projects and make them accessible from anywhere.

## Creating Google Mashups with the Google Mashup Editor

The Google Mashup Editor (GME) is an online development environment for creating mashups – web applications that draw data from various sources, process it, and present it in novel ways. In this book you will:

* Become familiar with the GME environment and learn about the gm: tags that underpin Google mashup applications.

* Learn core techniques for reading and writing data feeds, for handling events, and for utilizing the JavaScript API.

* Review example GME applications devised by the Google team and others, and develop a comprehensive case study application.

* Make mashups available by publishing them, embedding in web pages, and distributing as Google Gadgets.

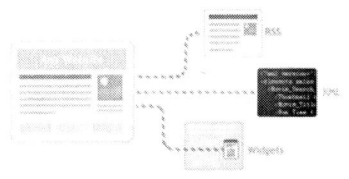

**ISBN-13:** 978-0-9556764-7-5
**ISBN-10:** 0955676479

## Mashups Made Easy with Dapper

Dapper offers a simple, accessible approach to web content 'mashup' development. It is a free-to-use, online mashup creation tool that requires only a web browser and no software downloads.

This book assumes no prior knowledge of Dapper, yet by the end you will be able to develop complex feature-rich mashups that utilize Dapper alone, or Dapper in conjunction with other mashup technologies like Microsoft Popfly, Yahoo Pipes, and the Google Mashup Editor.

"It is, by far, the most thorough tutorial anyone has ever written for Dapper and provides excellent step-by-step guides."

- Jon Aizen, Dapper CTO

# Index

CPSIA information can be obtained at www.ICGtesting.com
Printed in the USA
LVOW101629161011

250707LV00017B/240/P